From Adam to Moses

FROM ADAM TO MOSES

Harold W. Tribble

√Wayland

Convention Press

NASHVILLE   TENNESSEE

Copyright, 1934
The Sunday School Board
of the
Southern Baptist Convention
Nashville, Tenn.

Reprinted, 1959
Convention Press

511-00202

Library of Congress Catalog Card Number: 59-9308

Printed in the United States of America
15. AL 59 R.R.D.

About the Author

HAROLD WAYLAND TRIBBLE was born November 18, 1899 in Charlottesville, Virginia. He is the son of Henry Wise and Estelle Carlton (Rawlings) Tribble.

He holds the A.B. degree from Richmond College (now the University of Richmond). In 1922 he received the Th.M. degree from Southern Baptist Theological Seminary, Louisville, Kentucky, and in 1925 the Th.D. from the same seminary. He holds the M.A. degree from the University of Louisville (1927) and Ph.D. from the University of Edinburgh, Scotland (1937). Dr. Tribble studied at the University of Bonn, Germany (1931) and at the University of Basel, Switzerland (1936). He received the honorary D.D. degree from Stetson University (1930); LL.D. degrees from Union University (1939); Wake Forest College (1948); University of Richmond (1949); Duke University (1952); and University of North Carolina (1952).

He was ordained to the Baptist ministry in 1919. He served as assistant professor of theology at Southern Baptist Theological Seminary (1925–29) and as professor of theology at the same institution (1929–1947). From 1947–50 he served as president of Andover Newton Theological School, Newton Centre, Massachusetts, and in 1950 became president of Wake Forest College.

Dr. Tribble is a member of Kappa Sigma, Tau Kappa Alpha, and Old Town Club of Winston-Salem, North Carolina. He is the author of *Our Doctrines, Salvation,* and FROM ADAM TO MOSES. In 1935 he revised *The Baptist Faith* by E. Y. Mullins.

On June 10, 1925, he married Nelle Futch. They have three children: Harold Wayland, Jr., Betty May (Mrs. Richard Barnett), and Barbara Ann (Mrs. Harvey R. Holding).

Contents

Church Study Course for Teaching and Training

THE CHURCH STUDY COURSE for Teaching and Training began October 1, 1959. It is a merger of three courses previously promoted by the Baptist Sunday School Board—the Sunday School Training Course, the Graded Training Union Study Course, and the Church Music Training Course.

The course is fully graded. The system of awards provides a series of five diplomas of twenty books each for Adults or Young People, one diploma of ten books for Young People, two diplomas of five books each for Intermediates, and two diplomas of five books each for Juniors. All book awards earned previously in the Sunday School Training Course, the Graded Training Union Study Course, and the Church Music Training Course may be transferred to the new course.

The course is comprehensive, with books grouped into nineteen categories. The purpose of the course is to (1) help Christians to grow in knowledge and conviction; (2) help them grow toward maturity in Christian character and competence for service; (3) encourage them to participate worthily as workers in their churches; and (4) develop leaders for all phases of church life and work.

The Church Study Course for Teaching and Training is promoted by the Baptist Sunday School Board, 127 Ninth Avenue, North, Nashville, Tennessee, through its Sunday School, Training Union, Church Music, and Church Administration departments, and by these same departments in the states affiliated with the Southern Baptist Convention. A complete description of the course and the system of awards may be found in the *Church Study Course for Teaching and Training* catalog which may be obtained without charge from any one of these departments.

A record of all awards should be maintained in each church. A person should be designated by the church to keep the files. Forms for such records may be ordered from any Baptist Book Store.

Requirements for Credit in Class or Home Study

IF CREDIT is desired for the study of this book in a class or by home study, the following requirements must be met:

I. IN CLASSWORK

1. The class must meet a minimum of seven and one-half clock hours. The required time does not include assembly periods. Ten class periods of forty-five minutes each are recommended. (If laboratory or clinical work is desired in specialized or technical courses, this requirement may be met by six clock hours of classwork and three clock hours of supervised laboratory or clinical work.)

2. A class member who attends all class sessions and completes the reading of the book within a week following the last class session will not be required to do any written work.

3. A class member who is absent from one or more sessions must answer the questions on all chapters he misses. In such a case, he must turn in his paper within a week and must certify that the book has been read.

4. The teacher should request an award for himself. A person who teaches a book in sections B, C, or D of any category or conducts an approved unit of instruction for Nursery, Beginner, or Primary children will be granted an award in category 11, Special Studies, which will count as an elective on his own diploma. He should specify in his request the name of the book taught, or the unit conducted for Nursery, Beginners, or Primaries.

5. The teacher should complete the Request for Book Award—Class Study (Form 150) and forward it within two weeks after the completion of the class to the Church Study Course Awards Office, 127 Ninth Avenue, North, Nashville 3, Tennessee.

II. IN HOME STUDY

1. A person who does not attend any class session may receive credit by answering all questions for written work as indicated in the book. When a person turns in his paper on home study, he must certify that he has read the book.

2. Students may find profit in studying the text together, but individual papers are required. Carbon copies or duplicates in any form cannot be accepted.

3. Home study work papers may be graded by the pastor or a person designated by him, or they may be sent to the Church Study Course Awards Office for grading. The form Request for Book Award—Home Study (Form 151) must be used in requesting awards. It should be mailed to Church Study Course Awards Office, 127 Ninth Avenue, North, Nashville 3, Tennessee.

III. CREDIT FOR THIS BOOK

This book is in category 2, section A.

Suggested Audio-Visual Materials

FOR USE IN TEACHING THIS BOOK

The following audio-visual materials will be helpful in teaching this book. More material is listed than it will be practical to use. Select the slides, frames of the filmstrips, and the portions of motion pictures that contribute directly to the chapter you are teaching and that more nearly meet the needs of your group.

Chapter 1

SLIDES: *Ha 54* God Created All Things; *Ha 55*, Adam and Eve Driven Out of Paradise; *Ha 596*, Noah and His Sons Building the Ark; *Ha 56*, The Rainbow of Promise

FILMSTRIP: *In The Beginning*

MOTION PICTURES: *Creation According to Genesis; God of Creation*

Chapter 2

SLIDES: *Ha 598*, The Call of Abram; *Ha 599*, Abram Builds an Altar to God; *Ch 809*, Rubens—Flight of Lot

FILMSTRIP: *Abraham's Faith*

MOTION PICTURES: *Abraham's Faith; Abraham, Man of Faith*

Chapter 3

SLIDES: *N 12*, The Meeting of Rebekah and Isaac; *Ha 605*, Esau Sells His Birthright to Jacob

FILMSTRIP: *Abraham's Faith*

MOTION PICTURES: *Abraham, Man of Faith; Abraham's Faith*

Chapter 4

SLIDES: *Ha 605*, Esau Sells His Birthright to Jacob; *Ha 609*, Jacob Purges His Family of Strange Gods; *Hc 489*, Jacob's Ladder

MOTION PICTURE: *Jacob, Bearer of The Promise*

Chapter 5

SLIDES: *Ha 608*, Esau Forgives Jacob; *Ha 610*, Joseph's Dream; *Ha 611*, Jacob Sends Joseph to See His Brothers; *Ha 612*, Joseph Sold by His Brothers

FILMSTRIPS: *Joseph Sold Into Egypt; The Story of Joseph, Part I*

MOTION PICTURE: *Joseph, the Young Man*

Chapter 6

SLIDES: *N 19*, Joseph in Prison; *N 20*, Joseph the Ruler; *Ha 615*, Joseph Stores the Surplus Grain; *N 22*, Joseph and His Brothers; *Ha 617*, Joseph Meets Benjamin; *Ha 620*, Joseph Reveals Himself; *N 23*, Jacob and Joseph Meet; *Ha 621*, Joseph Brings Jacob Before Pharaoh

FILMSTRIP: *The Story of Joseph*—Part II

MOTION PICTURE: *Joseph, Ruler of Egypt*

Chapter 7

SLIDES: *N 25*, The Babe Among the Bulrushes; *N 26*, The Burning Bush; *Ha 624*, Moses and Aaron Before Pharaoh; *Ha 625*, The First Passover

FILMSTRIPS: Life of Moses Series; *A Baby Found; Moses Escapes to Midian; The Burning Bush*

MOTION PICTURES: *The Baby Moses; Moses, Called by God*

Chapter 8

SLIDES: *Ha 626*, Israelites Led by the Pillar of Cloud and Fire; *N 28*, The Crossing of the Red Sea; *Ha 628*, Bread Rains From Heaven; *Ha 629*, Moses Strikes the Rock for Water; *Ha 630*, The Israelites Come to Mount Sinai; *N 30*, The Law Given on Mount Sinai; *Ha 631*, God Speaks to the People of Israel

FILMSTRIPS: Life of Moses Series: *The Exodus; The Ten Commandments*

MOTION PICTURES: *Moses, Leader of God's People; The Red Sea*

Chapter 9

SLIDES: *N 31*, The Worship of The Golden Calf; *Ha 632*, Moses Pleads for Israel; *Ha 634*, The Tabernacle and the Pillar of Cloud; *Ha 635*, Gifts for The Tabernacle; *Ha 636*, The Tabernacle; *Ha 644*, Moses Teaching the People God's Commandments; *N 35*, The Death of Moses

FILMSTRIPS: Life of Moses Series: *The Tabernacle; The Death of Moses and Aaron*

MOTION PICTURE: *Moses, Leader of God's People*

CHAPTER 1

I. THE BOOK OF BEGINNINGS (Gen. 1:1–25)

II. ADAM THE GREAT (Gen. 1:25 to 2:25)
  1. Crown of God's Progressive Creation
  2. Different Method Employed in Man's Creation
  3. Made in God's Image
  4. The Home Established

III. ADAM THE SINNER (Gen. 3:1–7)
  1. Beginning of Human Sin
  2. Presence of the Tempter in the Garden
  3. The Way of Temptation and Sin

IV. ADAM THE SUFFERER (Gen. 3:8–24)
  1. Man the Slave of Guilt and Fear
  2. Physical, Mental, and Spiritual Suffering

V. CAIN THE MURDERER (Gen. 4)
  1. Brothers Characterized in the Act of Worship
  2. God Warns Cain
  3. Cain's Reaction
  4. Murder Committed and Denied

VI. ENOCH THE EXCEPTION (Gen. 5)
  1. Dreary Fifth Chapter
  2. Enoch Characterized by the Way He Walked

VII. NOAH THE RIGHTEOUS (Gen. 6:1 to 9:17)
  1. God Grieved at the Multiplication of Sin
  2. Why Sin Was Allowed
  3. The Flood Sent in Judgment

VIII. SHEM, FATHER OF THE SEMITES (Gen. 9:18 to 11:26)

1

Adam the First to the Beginning
of the Semitic Race

Genesis 1:1 to 11:26

I. THE BOOK OF BEGINNINGS (Gen. 1:1-25)

Genesis is a book of beginnings. That is what the name implies. The account starts with the very beginning of all things—"In the beginning God." If you try to go back beyond that you have only God; he had no beginning, for he is eternal. Beyond that also you have only eternity, for time started in the beginning, that is, in creation. And beyond that you have only spirit, for all material things began to exist in the creation. So the writer of Genesis starts his account with the very beginning of time and things—how far back that goes no one knows. The writer does not attempt to tell us; his chief concern is to show the presence and power and purpose of God in it all, and our chief concern should be to understand that. We are not seeking charts, maps, and schedules, but purposes that our God is bringing to realization in history.

Were you surprised to see the designation, "Adam the First," in the chapter heading? Perhaps you wondered about the meaning of the name. The writer of Genesis had three reasons for using the name Adam for the first man. First, it was the common word among the Hebrews for man as a being in distinction from animals. It referred to the race of man, including men and women. Often in the Old Testa-

1

ment we have the Hebrew word translated man, instead of Adam, for example, in Psalm 8:5 and Ezekiel 2:1, where the Hebrew word is the same that is used for Adam in the early chapters of Genesis. Second, the word in the original was kin to another word which meant ground, and which is used in Genesis 2:7. The third reason for using this word was that it was kin to yet another term that refers to likeness, and that occurs in Genesis 1:26. So when Moses wrote of Adam he was thinking of the first man, the first human being, who was made out of the dust of the ground, and in the likeness of God.

II. ADAM THE GREAT (Gen. 1:25 to 2:25)

What is the theme of the first two chapters of Genesis? What relation do these chapters have to the rest of the story that is unfolded in the Bible? Do they have a message for us today? Or, are they merely ancient history? We shall answer these and other similar questions with greater clarity if we keep in mind the fact that man is the central figure in all of God's creation, and hence in this narrative.

1. *Crown of God's Progressive Creation*

God created progressively, with man in view as the climax of his work. He had first to bring order out of chaos, something in orderly arrangement out of nothing. This he did, dividing the light from darkness, establishing the atmospheric conditions and clouds that surround the earth, separating the continents from the oceans, and commanding the land to bring forth plant life. The stars and planets were established in their orbits; the seas were filled with fish; birds of all varieties were made to fly in the air; the earth was filled with all the species of animal life; and to all plant and animal life was given the power of growth and reproduction. Lastly, God made man. Up the ascending scale of creation the Maker of all things came, until he approached the climax of all of his work, man. When we think of Adam as the accomplishment of God's greatest purpose in creative activity and as possessing the capacities and potentialities that make man what he is today, we begin to appreciate his greatness.

The first verse in Genesis tells us that God is the Creator of all things. "In the beginning God created." There the Bible starts, and there the Bible rests its case in the matter of accounting for the origin of the universe and life. The name for God that is used here suggests infinite power, and surely it required unlimited power to do the work of creation. God is also spoken of as spirit—"And the Spirit of God moved upon the face of the waters" (Gen. 1:2).[1] The New Testament teaches that all things were created through the eternal Christ (see John 1:3; Col. 1:16; and Heb. 1:2). Thus God as he is revealed to us throughout the Bible was active in creation. The point is not whether the Genesis account of creation teaches the doctrine of the Trinity, but that all the revelation of God adds meaning to his work in creation. The same God who created all things is man's Redeemer.

2. Different Method Employed in Man's Creation

Three features distinguished the making of man from the rest of God's creative work. The first was the divine council and decree: "God said, Let us make man." The second was the divine type after which he was formed: "Let us make man in our image, after our likeness" (Gen. 1:26). The third feature was the fact that God created him immediately. In producing other forms of life God had simply said, "Let the waters bring forth," or, "Let the earth bring forth;" but now he says, "Let us make man." So also there were three stages in the creation of man: (1) "And the Lord God formed man of the dust of the ground"; (2) "and breathed into his nostrils the breath of life"; (3) "and man became a living soul" (Gen.

2:7). These stages were not necessarily set apart in three separate periods of time. They were merely separate phases of God's work in creating man.

3. *Made in God's Image*

The chief thing for us to notice about man's creation is that he was made in the image of God. That accounts for his position with reference to all the rest of creation. He has dominion over all the earth. The wondrous things that we are doing through science today are made possible because man bears in himself the image of God. That accounts also for the immortality of the soul, for to be made in the image of God is to be made capable of unending fellowship with him.

4. *The Home Established*

It was not enough that man should be made to live above the animals and below God; he must be capable of building a home and reproducing the human family upon the earth. And so God made mankind of opposite sexes, male and female, man and woman. He made each for the other and so ordained marriage and the home. "Therefore shall a man leave his father and his mother, and shall cleave unto his wife: and they shall be one flesh" (Gen. 2:24). Here we have the establishment of a principle that runs all the way through history and society. Marriage and the home are ordained of God, planted in the very foundation of human life for the accomplishment of his wise and good purposes. They are not of man's design and making and therefore are not to be set aside by him, but are to be kept sacred and under God's control.

III. ADAM THE SINNER (Gen. 3:1–7)

As in the first section we studied the beginning of human life, so now we trace the beginning of human sin.

1. *Beginning of Human Sin*

Man was surrounded with all the blessings that could come through creation. Everything was designed for his happiness: he had work to do, and the earth was rich in resources for him to develop; he had abundant provisions for food, shelter, and clothing as he found need for them; and he had fellowship with God. Surely he should have been content in serving God in this happy relationship!

2. *Presence of the Tempter in the Garden*

But the tempter was there. Where he came from and when he came into being the story does not relate. And that suggests that the purpose of the account is not to settle speculative questions, such as "Where did the devil come from?" but to give practical guidance in solving the problem of sin. Where evil came from we may not know, but that we have it with us we cannot doubt. Recognizing its presence we must seek to understand its nature. Other passages in the Bible lead us to believe that this tempter who seduced Adam and Eve was Satan, the devil (Rom. 16:20; Rev. 12:9; 20:2).

3. *The Way of Temptation and Sin*

The story of the beginning of sin in the first family is the story of the propagation of sin in every family and in every human life. Notice how the tempter approached Eve. Did he say to her, "God has been wondrously good to you in giving you so many things to make your life happy"? He did not. He said something like this: "Has not God limited your freedom here by holding something back from you?"

When the woman replied that God had warned them that if they should break his commandment they would die, the tempter went on to say that they would not die, but that God was denying them some privilege which should bring them great pleasure. There are the first two steps in the temptation that wrought the downfall of man. The first was the awakening of the desire for something more than God had permitted. It was unholy ambition, the desire for something that did not rightfully belong to man. The second step was doubting the goodness and justice of God. Eve was led to believe that God was deliberately keeping her and her husband in an unhappy condition of limitation, whereas if she would disobey his will she would enter into a freedom through experience that she could not have otherwise.

Then followed the third step in yielding to temptation, which was meditating upon the thing that the tempter was holding out to her, dreaming of the pleasures of sin: "And . . . the woman saw that the tree was good for food"— hunger for the unrighteous satisfaction of physical appetite—; "and that it was a delight to the eyes"—attractive and alluring indulgence of vanity—; "and that the tree was to be desired to make one wise"—promising greater knowledge through the experience of evil (Gen. 3:6). That is not simply the story of the first temptation. It is the statement of the principle on which all temptation works. It is the same way that Satan tried to accomplish the downfall of Jesus at the beginning of his ministry. It is the same way that temptation comes to every one of us today.

Then came the climax of temptation, the act of sin. Eve and her husband broke God's commandment together. Individual sin immediately became social sin. One sin is no sooner committed than another is begun, and so it multiplies until a network of evil envelops the life that yields to temptation. That has been the experience of every sinner.

IV. ADAM THE SUFFERER (Gen. 3:8–24)

The writer does not leave the account with the beginning of sin, but goes on to tell of its results and the beginning of suffering.

1. *Man the Slave of Guilt and Fear*

Notice some of the results of the first sin. The man and his wife hid themselves from God because they were afraid. The disobedience that they had thought would bring them delightful experience and new freedom actually made them the slaves of guilt and fear. The cowards that they became, they tried to run away from God! The second result was their unwillingness to confess blame. The man blamed it on the woman, and the woman blamed it on the tempter. But all of them had to endure the consequences of sin.

2. *Physical, Mental, and Spiritual Suffering*

All of the consequences of sin may be summed up in this one word, suffering. Physical suffering came to the man in many burdens that would beset him in maintaining his existence upon the earth and to the woman in bearing her children. Mental suffering came to both in the haunting fear that would always be their lot as they tried to hide their sins from God. Social suffering would be their increasing portion as their family grew, for there would be disharmony between the man and the woman, and that would be reproduced in the children.

But their greatest suffering was spiritual. Sin inevitably brought on a separation from God that meant a godless life for man. When God told the man and the woman that if they sinned against him they would die, he was warning them against this spiritual separation, for that is death. He told them, in effect, that sin would drive them out of his presence. And it came to pass even as he had told them.

The result of sin has ever been suffering and death. All the way from the sin of the first man in the Garden of Eden to the atoning death of the Son of man on Calvary's cross, sin has left its stream of suffering. "By one man sin entered into the world, and death by sin" (Rom. 5:12).

V. CAIN THE MURDERER (Gen. 4)

If in the last episode of the story of Adam and Eve we saw the beginning of suffering, here we see the beginning of social crime, or the rapid spread of sin and its consequences in the family of man.

1. *Brothers Characterized in the Act of Worship*

Cain and Abel were brothers in the first family, but they were different. Both of them sought to worship God with an offering, but Abel had faith (see Heb. 11:4), whereas Cain was content with a less spiritual act. It became evident that God accepted with favor the offering that Abel brought, while he did not approve Cain's act of worship. In the reaction of Cain to that discrimination, we see the seed of murder working in his heart. Jealousy, envy, anger,—the sins of the heart—began upsetting him and giving him an ugly outlook on life. He began to imagine that his troubles were all caused by his brother.

2. *God Warns Cain*

It was at this stage that God came to Cain to warn him and to help him to resist his temptation. While the storm clouds of envy, jealousy, and anger were gathering in his heart, Jehovah warned him concerning the nature of sin and the way to overcome it. He said something like this: "Why are you angry and downcast? Do you not know that if you do the good thing you will have the joy of true excellence? On the other hand, if you do not do that which is right, sin is at the door of your life. Now the thing to do is to conquer it while it is only a desire in your heart, otherwise it will conquer you." God is ever coming to the sinner to warn him about his sin, to help him to keep from sinning, for he is "not willing that any should perish, but that all should come to repentance" (2 Peter 3:9).

3. *Cain's Reaction*

The way Cain reacted to God's warning is the way sin grows in human hearts. If he had accepted the advice that came to him and had prayed to the Lord for help to overcome the evil spirit in his heart, he would not have committed murder. But instead of doing that he went out and talked with Abel, and it was the kind of talk that led to murder. While Cain talked, the spirit of jealousy was smoldering in his heart, and the more he said the more envious and angry he became, until in a fit of rage he struck his own brother dead.

4. *Murder Committed and Denied*

And so on the earliest pages of human history, sin left its ugliest mark, premeditated murder. It would seem that Adam's sin was little in comparison, but it was the seed of which Cain's was the fruit. As long as man obeys God he is able to overcome sin, but when he chooses the path of wilful disobedience he becomes the victim of evil. Cain killed his own brother who was a good man. He did it in the face of God's warning, and so it was an act of wilful sin against God. He did it because his heart was filled with an evil spirit. When we ask why Cain murdered Abel, 1 John 3:12 answers, "Because his works were evil, and his brother's righteous." Murder is an ugly fruit that grows on the tree of sin, a tree that has its roots deep in the spirit of jealousy, envy, anger, and other ungodly emotions that stir in the secret places of the human heart.

When God came to Cain after he had committed his great sin, he tried, like Adam and Eve, to escape the judgment. He said he did not know where his brother was, but of course he did know. Then, in a bad temper, he said, "Am I my brother's keeper?" Whether he intended to or not, he touched upon the central principle that should always keep man from murder.

We are all brothers in the sense that we are created by the same God, for the same purpose of serving God in happy fellowship. Each is his brother's keeper, the custodian of the welfare of every other man, and therefore murder is a sin against God and the social order that he has established.

When God pronounced his judgment, Cain became frightened lest someone should kill him. Cowardice, self-interest, fear—these are ever the companions of sin in the heart of the unrighteous. Cain went forth from the presence of God—the first fugitive and murderer in the earth.

VI. Enoch the Exception (Gen. 5)

Following the account of Cain's great sin and its consequences, there is a recital of the "vital statistics" of the descendants of Adam as far as Noah.

1. *Dreary Fifth Chapter*

The record varies only in names and numbers, with the exception of Enoch. There was no significant difference in the circumstances under which all these characters lived, yet Enoch lived a different life. It was a difference that was the result of diligently meeting the conditions on which man may have fellowship with God. We are not told that all of the others listed were extremely sinful; in fact, there is nothing said of them except that they were born, lived, and died.

2. *Enoch Characterized by the Way He Walked*

Enoch was the exception to the rule because he "walked with God." That is a phrase that characterizes the religious life, the life of devotion to God. It is used twice here in the brief statement about Enoch. It indicates continued faith in God and obedience to his will. That is the interpretation that the writer of Hebrews puts upon it (Heb. 11:5). Walking with God means harmonious relationship with him, loving what he loves, seeing life from his point of view, seeking to do his will in every experience of life. "Can two walk together, except they be agreed?" (Amos 3:3).

Walking with God indicates progress in fellowship with him. When a man walks he goes somewhere, and when he walks with someone he goes somewhere with his companion; they grow in friendship. And so while others were merely living and dying, Enoch was growing in the fellowship with God that is life eternal. When his time came to die, this unusual man did not have to go the way others went, but "God took him." "By faith Enoch was translated that he should not see death" (Heb. 11:5). A little girl is reported to have told it in these words: "God was accustomed to take walks with Enoch, and one day they went further than usual, and God said, 'Enoch, you are a long way from home; better come in and stay with me'; and so he went, and has stayed ever since."

VII. Noah the Righteous (Gen. 6:1 to 9:17)

The law of sin is the law of multiplication. From little to more it grows until it would seem to be beyond all reach and calculation.

1. God Grieved at the Multiplication of Sin

In the days of Noah "God saw that the wickedness of man was great in the earth, and that every imagination of the thoughts of his heart was only evil continually." Sin everywhere! Had God done right in creating man? It seems that he raised that question as he looked upon the wickedness of his greatest creature, "And it repented the Lord that he had made man on the earth, and it grieved him at his heart." Over in the New Testament we are told to "grieve not the Holy Spirit of God" (Eph. 4:30). The simple story of the whole Bible is that the heart of our Heavenly Father is grieved by our sin. He made us for a better life than that of sinfulness.

2. Why Sin Was Allowed

Would it not have been better, someone asks, if God had made man incapable of choosing sin? Then there would have been no sin to grieve him. But neither would there have been any voluntary and faithful worship to please him. If there is no opportunity for a Cain to develop, there is also no opportunity for an Enoch to walk with God by faith. God created man for righteousness, but man must have the power of choosing between obedience and disobedience if his righteousness is to be of the highest type. It was God's desire from the first that his creature should choose the path of righteous service and fellowship.

3. The Flood Sent in Judgment

God's purpose in creation was frustrated by sin. What was God to do? Surely he could not stand aside and allow sin to run its course until it had completely destroyed the family of man from the face of the earth! His holy nature cried out in protest. Sin should be judged and destroyed, and the righteous should be protected.

Was God just in bringing the flood to destroy sinful man? The answer lies in the history of his treatment of his creature before this event. He had given Adam and Eve clear instruction about the consequences of sin; had warned Cain before he murdered Abel; had called Enoch to walk by his side; had counseled with Noah; and with all of them he had walked frequently that, in his wonderful presence, righteousness might become attractive to them. But now he says, "My spirit shall not always strive with man" (Gen. 6:3). In other words, God's Spirit strives with man as long as there is any hope of saving him, until in the depth of sin he literally drives God away.

Through the flood God preserved Noah and his family, and the animals that they took with them into the ark. All men and beasts left on the outside were destroyed. Then, after many days, the waters receded and the occupants disembarked on dry land to begin life anew. Noah's first act was a good omen. He built an altar and worshiped the Lord. God was pleased and pledged that he would never again destroy the earth with a flood, and as a sign of his promise he put the rainbow in the clouds.

VIII. SHEM, FATHER OF THE SEMITES (Gen. 9:18 to 11:26)

After the account of Noah's life we have another long list of generations, given evidently to show the accomplishment of God's purpose through history. Noah had three sons, Shem, Ham, and Japheth. Shem was chosen to receive the special favor of the Lord. The other two were to be subordinate to him. In the line of Shem's descendants came Abraham, who became the father of the Hebrews.

In his desire to produce a new and better race of men, God began to prepare for the coming of his Son to redeem the world from sin. Jesus was born a Jew, a Semite, but he became the Saviour of the world, that in him all the races and nations might become one family in the kingdom of God.

FOR CLASS DISCUSSION OR FURTHER STUDY

1. Why does the author characterize Adam as "the Great"? Do you agree with this classification?
2. Point out the progress of temptation in the experience of Eve. Compare her experience with that of any tempted human being.
3. What do we learn from Cain's response to God's warning? What was the result of Cain's sin in his own life?
4. What do the Bible genealogies in Genesis show about the kinship of all people?

---

[1] Scripture quotations in this textbook are from the American Standard Version, or the King James Version unless otherwise stated.

CHAPTER 2

I. ABRAM A SEMITE (Gen. 11:27-32)

    1. His Place in the Plan of Redemption
    2. Civilization in Ur

II. BLESSED TO BLESS (Gen. 12:1-3)

    1. Ready When God Called
    2. Called to Follow God's Leading
    3. Blessed that He Might Become a Blessing

III. BECOMES A DECEIVER (Gen. 12:4 to 13:4)

    1. Habit of Worship
    2. Shechem and Bethel
    3. Sin in Egypt
    4. Becomes Prosperous

IV. BREAKS WITH LOT (Gen. 13:5 to 16:16)

    1. Peril of Riches
    2. Friction in the Family
    3. Abram's Unselfishness and Lot's Selfishness
    4. Rescues Lot and Meets Melchizedek
    5. Birth of Ishmael

V. BEGINNING OF THE COVENANT (Gen. 17:1-14)

    1. Abram Becomes Abraham
    2. Covenant Established
    3. Rite of Circumcision

VI. BIRTH OF ISAAC (Gen. 17:15 to 22:24)

    1. Sarai Becomes Sarah
    2. Destruction of Sodom and Gomorrah
    3. Isaac Born and Named
    4. Abraham's Faith Tested, Isaac Presented to God

VII. ESTIMATE OF ABRAHAM

Abraham

Genesis 11:27 to 22:24

Who was Abraham and who were his people? Why does he hold such a prominent place in early Bible history? What do we know about the time and the countries in which he lived? Why did he move about so much? And what significance does all of this have for us today? Our minds bristle with questions when we think of this ancient patriarch. Perhaps all of them will not be answered here, but we should take them with us to a fresh study of Genesis. And even as we are attempting to answer the ones that have been raised others will occur to us.

I. ABRAM A SEMITE (Gen. 11:27–32)

Abram and his people were Semites, descendants of Shem, as were many of the people among whom he moved in his travels. We recall that Shem was one of the sons of Noah, and Noah was the righteous man with whom God began to build a better race upon the earth after the flood. God chose Shem and his descendants to receive his special blessings, and now Abram comes into that line of promise.

1. *His Place in the Plan of Redemption*

Abram's connection with the purpose of God was more important than his connection by blood with Shem, for that purpose included the revelation of God and the redemption of man. All that was done in succeeding generations toward the achievement of that twofold purpose was involved in the relation between God and Abram.

Here we may begin to reckon time and dates. The other events that we have been studying occurred in history, but they are rather obscured in primitive times, and we have no reliable mileposts by which to chart the dates and the years. But with Abram we come into the realm of dated history.

2. Civilization in Ur

Abram lived about 2000 B.C., in Ur, in southern Babylonia, between the Euphrates and Tigris rivers. It was a favorable position for the development of commerce and civilization. Ur was the chief city of all that country, as well as one of the oldest, having come to the peak of its glory as early as 3500 B.C. It was the seat of the worship of the moon god Nannar or Sin, whose massive temple stood seventy feet above the plain.

Much valuable archaeological research work has been done in the region of Ur,[1] the results of which indicate that the civilization of Abram's day was old and well advanced. Writing was practiced, governments were well founded, the arts were studied, and the people engaged in extended commerce. Cities had been established and kings reigned thousands of years before Abram's day. Down in Egypt, whither he went, the pyramids were already hoary with age, symbols of an earlier civilization that extended many centuries into the past.

II. BLESSED TO BLESS (Gen. 12:1–3)

With civilizations advancing, business developing, people building cities, why should God call a man to do something different? Why not let the world go on its way and take the consequences, whatever they might be? Because God had something better in view than the world by itself could possibly realize. His desire was to reveal himself to man, for he knew full well that man would never come to know him in righteous fellowship without revelation. His desire was also to redeem man from the sin that was ever carrying him deeper into destruction. The people all around Abram were worshiping idols, and usually idolatry carried with it many forms of immorality. The descendants of Shem had gone in the ways of the people of the days of Noah, and a new beginning must be made. Only this time it would not be a plan involving the destruction of many, but the cultivation of covenant relations with a chosen few. God must choose one man with whom to make the start.

1. Ready When God Called

But why did he choose Abram, rather than someone else? Because here was a man, like Enoch in an earlier period, who was ready. While others were indulging in unseemly practices before images of wood and stone, he was seeking the quiet places where he could commune with the eternal Spirit. Across many generations the story of Noah's righteousness had been handed along from father to son, and Abram was cherishing the hope and determination and the prayer that he might be something like his illustrious ancestor. One thing he determined to do: he would walk with God.

How did God call him? Was it a voice that was audible to his physical ears? Or was it the inaudible message of the Spirit to his soul that came in the quiet time of meditation? What difference does it make how it came, so long as it came to him from God? Wherever a man is ready to listen and obey, God is ready and able to make his will known. Did the Lord reveal everything to Abram at once? On the contrary, God led him step by step. He told him enough at the first to let him know that he had a special purpose for his life, and that he would guide him and protect him until the accomplishment of that purpose, as far as it could be achieved in his lifetime. That was enough for the beginning, but to enable God to work out his plan it was necessary for Abram to leave his people and go to a different land. After that, as he needed new assurance and new guidance, his God was at hand to speak to him and to steady him.

2. Called to Follow God's Leading

Where did God tell Abram to go? "Unto the land that I will show thee" (Gen. 12:1). He did not let him know at first what the end of his journey would be, but he let him know unmistakably that he must leave his home country and kindred. They were worshipers of idols, and their influence on him would tend to hinder the growth of the knowledge of the true God. He would not lose by leaving home. His God would provide for him, would make him great. There is always an abundant recompense for all that God calls upon us to give up. Jesus said that if we leave father or mother, houses or land, for his sake, the reward will be a hundred fold here and life everlasting beyond. If he commands one, "Sell that which thou hast," the promise is, "Thou shalt have treasure in heaven" (Matt. 19:21). So it is ever true that God is mindful of our needs when he calls us to follow him.

God's call is not to every one to leave home, but it is to every one to follow him. It may be to some to go back home and witness for him, as Jesus told the healed Gadarene demoniac. But Abram must go, and he went, taking his wife and Lot, his nephew, and his servants and possessions with him. It was a day of such travel, and so he probably did not attract much notice. There were many who traveled from place to place, making their homes wherever they chanced to stop. They sought better pasturage, better opportunities for making money, more food, or more places of amusement in the cities. Abram was different. The unseen hand of the all-wise God rested gently upon his heart, guiding him here and there, not aimlessly but with a purpose that embraced the blessings of heaven for the children of men for untold generations to come. What a journey was begun here! More important than the voyage of Columbus! The redemption of a world was in the balance when this patriarch of seventy-five started toward the western world.

3. Blessed that He Might Become a Blessing

He was to be God's medium of blessings. "I will bless thee, . . . and thou shalt be a blessing" (Gen. 12:2). God would form a covenant with him, which would later be confirmed in Moses, and which would embrace a great nation. Jews and Christians alike date their commission to serve the living God from the call of Abram. It is a missionary challenge that should never be forgotten. Jesus interpreted the promise to Abram as fulfilled in himself.

III. BECOMES A DECEIVER (Gen. 12:4 to 13:4)

1. Habit of Worship

What was the first thing that Abram did when he stopped at a new place to sojourn awhile? What is the first thing that you do when you move to a place where you are not known? His custom was to erect an altar and worship God. We are not stretching matters when we say that wherever he established his home he also established his church relationship— a splendid example for Christians to follow today.

2. Shechem and Bethel

His first stop was at Shechem. It was here that his grandson dug a well some years later, and that his greatest descendant talked with a Samaritan woman about the way of life. Then he journeyed on to Bethel, where he built another altar. Bethel means "House of God," the place where God is found and worshiped. This place was to figure in Abram's experience again, and it was to hold a larger place in Jacob's religious life.

Abram did not tarry at Bethel, for there was a famine in the land. There was grass in Egypt, not too far away, and so he journeyed toward the south. When he entered Egypt he broke his rule of faith, failing to erect his altar of worship. It was a good thing to do at Shechem and at Bethel, and it would have been equally wise in the land of the Pharaohs. If he had adhered to his habit of public worship in strange lands, the account of his life would have been different. He was faithful in the great issues of life, but fearful in some of the circumstances in connection with a journey. He would pitch his whole life on faith in the promise of God, but he was afraid to trust the Lord in a mere detail of that promise.

3. Sin in Egypt

Why did he lie about Sarai, and ask her to say that she was his sister instead of his wife? (She was, in fact, his half sister before he married her, but it was a lie nevertheless to say that she was not his wife.) She was a beautiful woman, and he was afraid that some of the Egyptians would fall in love with her and kill him in order to get her as wife. Surely that is cowardice going to an extreme! And there is no indication that he had any idea of trying to redeem her later. He would sacrifice her to save himself. The great man of faith is not very great here. But we must not judge him by the standards of the twentieth century. Although it was wrong then, and not to be condoned, yet woman was not held on the high level of esteem that she enjoys today.

When Pharaoh discovered his mistake he sent for Abram and said, "What is this that thou hast done unto me? why didst thou not tell me that she was thy wife? . . . now therefore behold thy wife, take her, and go thy way" (Gen. 12:18-19). And he was sent away with his wife and possessions, judged unfaithful by a man who made no pretense to faith in Jehovah. What a pity! A believer rebuked by an unbeliever! Abram had an opportunity to witness for the true God before Pharaoh and the Egyptians, but he lost it through his moral failure and was sent away in disgrace. How often that has happened when Christians have been lacking in faithfulness and steadfastness in their dealings with people outside the church! Christianity is always discounted by an unbelieving world when professing Christians compromise morally with the world.

4. *Becomes Prosperous*

But God did not cast Abram off because he slipped. Here is a splendid example of divine forbearance with man in his weakness. Abram was allowed to become rich in spite of his faithlessness and because of the mercy of God. He was to learn, as all of us need to learn, that the only true prosperity comes on the basis of faithful obedience to God. Abram went back to Bethel, where he had built an altar, and there he worshiped God in confession of his sin and in reconsecration of his life.

IV. BREAKS WITH LOT (Gen. 13:5 to 16:16)

The peril of riches! Here is the first rich man mentioned in the Bible, and we no sooner hear of his riches than we must listen to the story of family dissension.

1. *Peril of Riches*

There are problems that are inevitably connected with accumulating wealth, as there are other problems that are a part of poverty; and they are never solved on the basis of selfishness, but in gracious forbearance and in the willingness to sacrifice self in the interest of others. How many times have families been divided over the question of the division of property! The story runs through history like an ugly scar that will not end. We would avoid many tragic blunders if we would read again the story of Abram and follow his example in such matters.

2. *Friction in the Family*

Lot had been with Abram in all of his travels, and had shared in the accumulation of his wealth. But now their growing flocks and herds required wider pasture ranges, and yet the two families were trying to keep together. It is not surprising that the servants quarreled. The herds were constantly getting mixed; Lot's shepherds would claim some of Abram's sheep, and Abram's servants would seek to bring back some of their master's wandering cattle, and a fight would ensue. From an occasional misunderstanding it grew until it became a daily affair.

3. *Abram's Unselfishness and Lot's Selfishness*

Abram was the older and the wealthier of the two, and the head of the family. He would have been acting within his rights according to the standards of the world if he had spoken harshly to Lot and told him to whip his servants into submission, or he would be held accountable. But instead of that Abram spoke kindly and unselfishly: "Let there be no strife, I pray thee, between me and thee, and between my herdsmen and thy herdsmen; for we are brethren. Is not the whole land before thee? separate thyself, I pray thee, from me: if thou wilt take the left hand, then I will go to the right; or if thou take the right hand, then I will go to the left" (Gen. 13:8-9). Let us inscribe those words indelibly upon our hearts and cherish them as a motto for all family, church, social, and industrial relations.

We would expect Lot to say, "Not so, Uncle Abram, for by all rights you should have first choice, and then I shall be glad to take what is left." But Lot was not that kind. Here were two different men, and a transaction involving money and property revealed the true character of each. Off toward the Jordan was a well-watered plain that reminded one of the fertile section of Egypt, which was clearly the better part of the land, and Lot unhesitatingly chose it. But he failed to consider seriously enough the dangers of living among the wicked people of the cities of the plain. His selfish choice affected the rest of his life; it was the beginning of tragedy for Lot and for all his family.

4. Rescues Lot and Meets Melchizedek

As a further indication of his love for Lot and his desire to protect him, Abram went to his rescue when he was taken prisoner in battle, and by skilful maneuvering and heroic boldness defeated his captors, and brought Lot and his family and property back to Sodom. It was as he was returning from this expedition that Melchizedek appeared to Abram and blessed him. Abram gave to him a tenth of his possessions, which fact indicates the antiquity of the law of the tithe, and is referred to by the author of the epistle to the Hebrews.

5. Birth of Ishmael

Once more God renewed his promise to his servant that he would make of his children a mighty nation. Abram believed and trusted Jehovah, but the fact remained that his first child had not yet been born. It had been ten years since he entered Canaan, and he and Sarai were getting old. She became discouraged and persuaded her husband to resort to a custom that was in vogue in that day and take another wife. He consented and took Sarai's maid Hagar, and a son was born to him by her, who received the name Ishmael. We may be tempted to criticize Abram again for his laxness, but it is to be remembered that it was the ordinary thing in those days for a man to have as many wives as he wanted and could support. In our day of civilization under the floodlight of the full revelation in Jesus Christ, we must adhere to loftier moral standards. Abram's first sin in this case was his failure to wait patiently and obediently for the will of Jehovah to be done.

V. BEGINNING OF THE COVENANT (Gen. 17:1-14)

1. Abram Becomes Abraham

Up to this time the grand old patriarch had been known as Abram, which means exalted father, but now his name was changed to Abraham, which means father of a multitude. By this new name he was to be known through the remainder of his life, and throughout history; it is the name that is immediately related to the establishment of the covenant.

2. Covenant Established

The covenant was a compact entered into between God and Abraham, in which each pledged to do certain things for the other. On his side God promised to bless Abraham, give him a family that would grow into a mighty multitude who should inherit the land of Canaan as an abiding possession, and he would always be their God. On the other side Abraham must pledge to walk before God in righteous obedience, and devote himself and all his family and descendants to the service of God.

3. Rite of Circumcision

All of the most binding covenants that the ancients made were sealed with blood, which was a symbol of the pledge of life to observe the conditions established. It was also a symbol of the commingling of the lives of those who entered into the covenant agreement. Circumcision, as the sign of this covenant, indicated that all of Abraham's descendants were included in the pledge that he made to God.

VI. BIRTH OF ISAAC (Gen. 17:15 to 22:24)

1. Sarai Becomes Sarah

Along with the change in Abraham's name in connection with the establishment of the covenant, his wife's name was also changed. Henceforth, she was to be known as Sarah, which means princess. She was to be the mother of kings, and princes, and nations. Jehovah was about to bestow a great blessing upon her. She was ninety years old, and her husband was ninety-nine when the Lord informed Abraham that she would give birth to the long-promised son, and she laughed because it seemed improbable to her according to the laws of nature. Abraham thought that perhaps the promise would yet be fulfilled in Ishmael, but God assured him that it would be through a son born to Sarah.

2. Destruction of Sodom and Gomorrah

It was about this time that an evil report came concerning the cities where Lot was living. The sin of Sodom and Gomorrah had become "very grievous," and God decided to destroy them. But Lot was there and therefore Abraham was deeply concerned. He interceded for the cities on behalf of Lot, but because there were not enough righteous people in them to justify God in sparing them, they were destroyed. Nevertheless, Lot and his family were given ample opportunity to escape, as a further evidence of God's interest in Abraham and in answer to his prayer, although only Lot and his two single daughters took the warning seriously enough to flee. They tarried a while in the little town of Zoar, and then took up their abode in a cave in the mountains. This is the last scene that the Bible gives us in the life of Lot. He left his uncle rich and selfish, choosing the way of ease and pleasure that leads to sin, and he came back to the hills poor and defeated. We leave him to live out his few remaining years with his daughters on a very low moral level.

3. Isaac Born and Named

Finally, the oft-given and long-cherished promise was fulfilled and Isaac was born to Sarah. She named him Isaac, which means "laughter," for she said, "God hath made me to laugh; every one that heareth will laugh with me" (Gen. 21 : 6). It was the laughter of joy over the extraordinary manifestation of God's favor upon her.

The home developed an atmosphere of happiness, which was marred only by the jealousy between Sarah and Hagar. But God had plans for both sons. To prevent further mixing, and to maintain a congenial home life for Isaac, they had to be separated, and so Hagar took her departure and reared her child in the wilderness.

4. *Abraham's Faith Tested, Isaac Presented to God*

It would seem that the faith of Abraham had been tested quite enough, but he was yet to endure the supreme trial of his life. His son, the gift of God and the child of promise, who had brought the laughter of joy into his home, now meant everything to him. His hope for making his family great in the earth centered in the boy. Just as the patient waiting of the years had come into a happy fruition, God said, "Take now thy son, thine only son, whom thou lovest, even Isaac, and get thee into the land of Moriah; and offer him there for a burnt-offering" (Gen. 22:2). What would you have done if you had been in the patriarch's place? Do not bother about criticizing God for asking Abraham to make a sacrifice of his son, for that was so common among the people of that day that Abraham would not think it strange. And one purpose in the whole experience was to teach the lesson that the children of the covenant should not follow the common practice of offering human sacrifices in religious worship. The strange part was that God who had given Isaac to him should now propose to take him away.

Such an experience presents a problem to many a parent today. God calls to the mission field an only son whom the father had planned to establish in business. A child who had brought sunshine to the home is claimed in death. Do the parents rebel, or trust and follow the Lord? Instead of criticizing, let us compare our experiences and faith with Abraham's.

His faith held up nobly as he deliberately gave back to God the child who symbolized all that Jehovah had given to him. What faith! The author of Hebrews says that Abraham believed that God would raise his son from the dead and give him back to him (Heb. 11:17-19). Doctor Sampey suggests that it might well have been in connection with this experience that the words of Jesus were based (John 8:56-58), that as he was called upon to sacrifice his son he received a revelation of the saving sacrifice that God purposed to make in his Son on behalf of the world. Would that our faith might be as steady and unquestioning and forward-looking as that of Abraham.

VII. ESTIMATE OF ABRAHAM

Now that we have traced the history of the man, what can we say in the way of a summary appreciation of his character? It is difficult to judge him fairly, for it is almost impossible for us to orient ourselves in the world of his day. He lived when only the faint gray streaks across the eastern sky foretokened the dawn of the day of revelation, while we live in the full light of the noontide of God's revelation. Before we grade him down in character, let us answer this question: Are we as far ahead of Abraham in personal faith and obedience as Christian civilization is ahead of that of his day?

At least four outstanding characteristics of Abraham are manifest from our study:

1. He pursued the promises of God. He was the first great traveler mentioned in the Bible, but he was not a tourist on pleasure or sight-seeing bent; he was urged on by the conviction that it was the will of God, and that God had a pur-

pose in it that meant good for many people. God promised to give him a land and a great people, and he followed the gleam of that promise.

2. He was a man of great faith, and became the father of the faithful (Gal. 3:29). He did not live to see the promise of God fulfilled in material possessions, for when he died he did not own a foot of ground except the cave that he had bought for a burial place, but he had faith in God that was accounted unto him for righteousness, and having that he possessed the spiritual fulfilment of every promise. Every true believer would rather be a man of strong faith than a man of great material wealth.

3. He was devout in prayer. His whole life was pitched on the plane of prayer. It was through prayer that he was called. It was through prayer that he was guided and sustained. It was through prayer that he interceded for Lot. And it was through prayer that the promises of God were given to him and kept before his mind.

4. He was a friend of God (see Isa. 41:8; 2 Chron. 20:7; and James 2:23). He walked and talked with God.

FOR CLASS DISCUSSION OR FURTHER STUDY

1. What was God's ultimate purpose in calling Abram?
2. What covenant did God make with Abraham?
3. Indicate four or more characteristics which made Abraham a man whom God could use, in spite of the wrong things he did.
4. Using a concordance, find New Testament passages that refer to Abraham. What conclusion do you reach regarding his prominence in New Testament writings?

---

[1] J. McKee Adams, *Biblical Backgrounds* (Nashville: Broadman Press, 1934), pp. 25ff.

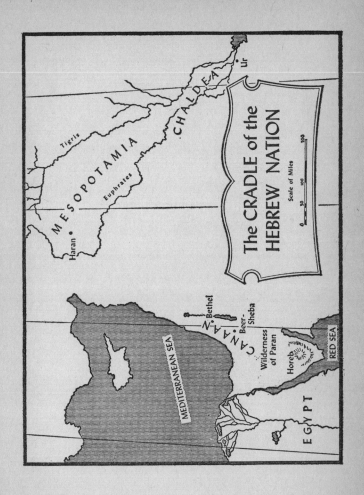

The CRADLE of the HEBREW NATION

Scale of Miles

0   50   100   150

MESOPOTAMIA

Tigris

Euphrates

Haran

CHALDEA

Ur

CANAAN

Bethel

Beer-Sheba

Wilderness of Paran

Horeb

MEDITERRANEAN SEA

EGYPT

RED SEA

CHAPTER 3

3

Isaac

Genesis 23:1 to 25:28; 26

I. THE DEATH OF SARAH (Gen. 23)

At the full age of one hundred and twenty-seven years
Sarah died. She is the only woman whose age is given in
the Bible. There is not much said about her in the accounts
that we have been studying; her character is delineated in
the background of the portrait of her famous husband, as
has been true of so many women since. She was a faithful
wife according to the standards of her day, carrying her
loyalty to her husband to the extreme of slavish obedience,
and counting her home her kingdom. Indeed, she left an
example of loyal devotion to her home that has influenced
Hebrew women throughout history.

She was too pretty for Abraham's comfort of mind at times,
and she carried her beauty and charm to a ripe old age. Her
good looks were responsible in part for Abraham's greatest
sins, for he was so afraid that other men would be attracted
by her charming appearance and would kill him to get her
that he lied about her twice, saying that she was not his wife
but his sister. And she was so faithful to him that she agreed
to the falsehood. Her treatment of Hagar showed her temper
and jealousy, but over every incident her loyalty to her husband and her home dominated her emotions and formed
her decisions. When she suggested that Abraham take Hagar
as a secondary wife she was lacking in faith in God, but she
was conscientious in accordance with the customs of her day.

As the mother of Isaac and a good mother in her home she became the mother of the faithful (1 Peter 3:6), as Abraham is regarded as the father of the faithful. That her husband and her son loved her devotedly in her life and grieved for her deeply in her death is made clear in the Genesis account.

II. BETROTHAL AND MARRIAGE OF ISAAC (Gen. 24)

After Sarah's death Abraham became concerned for Isaac, in whom the promises of God were to be carried forward toward realization. It would never do, he thought, to have him marry a Canaanite; a wife from his own cousins must be found, that the worship of Jehovah might not be endangered. Indeed, it would not be enough merely to procure one of his cousins for his wife, but special care must be exercised that a worthy successor of Sarah be found. The responsibility of being a channel of blessing to all the peoples of the earth was to descend from Abraham to Isaac as a precious birthright, and in this high calling his wife must share. She should possess all the high qualities and virtues indispensable for the fulfilment of that mission, for her position in the home as the mother of the children of promise was to be an important factor in the development of God's plans.

Here we have the first love story given in the Bible, and it is adorned with all the charm of ancient Oriental custom. The father took the lead in seeking a wife for his son, and Isaac was the dutiful and obedient type who quietly acquiesced in his father's desires. Two things the aged patriarch did to insure success: one was to entrust the task to a tried and faithful servant and friend; and the other was to pray for divine guidance and trust to God to bring the matter out according to his will. Abraham was content to rest his most cherished hope on those two scores. He was confident that Jehovah who called him from his native land with the promise of a great heritage, and who had given him his son in his old age, would send his angel before the servant to indicate the young woman who had been favored with God's choice.

This old servant set a fine example of faithfulness in line of duty. He prepared for the journey and started out with an undaunted faith that clearly marks him as a member of Abraham's household. Through the many years that he had traveled with his master he had learned to trust his God, and now he undertook this mission with very much the same resignation to divine guidance that Abraham exhibited when he left his native land and kindred for a land that was strange to him.

As the servant traveled, his thoughts were not of himself, but of his master and of the important task that had been committed to him. As he approached the city where the relatives lived, he paused to pray for special guidance. He was a wise man, as well as deeply religious, and he exhibited both characteristics in this prayer at the crisis of his undertaking. What would you have done in a similar circumstance? Would you have sought the help of friendly people in the vicinity who would know the family of Abraham's brother, or would you have asked for some miraculous sign?

Abraham's servant accepted the common situation that he was about to face, and simply asked that God would send the right woman to that place and that he might have sense enough to know her when she came along. His prayer being answered almost immediately, he insisted upon carrying his mission through to completion as soon as possible. He refused to eat until he had told his errand, and asked for Rebekah to be the wife of his master's son. And what an eloquent appeal he made! He told of his prayer and how God answered it by bringing Rebekah down to the well and letting him know that she was the one, and he rested the case on the confident assurance that God would bring about the desired result. No finer example of simple faith and implicit reliance upon divine guidance through prayer is to be found in all the Old Testament.

Too often we are prone to look with condescension upon one who is called a servant. We should remember that, in the full sense, he is a servant who ministers for another. This servant, who was in all probability the Eliezer of the fifteenth chapter of Genesis, was born in Abraham's household, and for many years had been given the responsibility of ruling over all of the other servants and all of Abraham's property. In fact, if Abraham had not had a son he would have inherited the estate (Gen. 15:2–3). Surely this servant was a noble man, worthy of all the trust that Abraham reposed in him!

No doubt this was the first word that Nahor and his family had heard directly from their kinsman who had left them on strange wanderings more than sixty-five years before. It was good to hear that he had been successful, had become wealthy, and had settled down and established a home. One can readily imagine that they had often talked about him and said something to the effect that a rolling stone gathers no moss, or that a wanderer seldom builds a fortune.

Laban noticed the ring that Eliezer had put in Rebekah's nose and the bracelets that he had put on her arms, and even as he was estimating their value his uncle's servant brought forth other costly presents: jewels of gold and silver and fine garments, gifts for every member of the family. They were impressed. Certainly Abraham knew his relatives when he started his servant forth on that trip! He was not to ask a favor but to bestow one when he asked for one of their daughters to become the bride of his son, and that is the impression that they got.

Rebekah was glad to go and become the wife of her cousin (she was Isaac's first cousin once removed), and her father and brother gave their consent; so after a short delay she and her maidservants started out with Eliezer on the return journey.

In the cool of the eventide, Isaac went out into the field to meditate. He probably had been praying every day that God might bless the servant and let him bring back a good and sensible cousin to be his wife, and as he lifted his eyes from his prayer he saw a camel train coming toward his home. Recognizing the servant, he went forward to meet him and to see his bride for the first time. But he was not to see her face until he had heard the full story of the providences of God that had made the journey successful. Rebekah lowered her veil and the servant recounted the events of the trip. Then Isaac brought her into his mother's tent, "and she became his wife; and he loved her: and Isaac was comforted after his mother's death" (Gen. 24:67). Was there ever a betrothal and marriage more completely consummated through faith and prayer? The circumstances vary, but the principle should always be the same for those who have faith in God. Surely the important matter of finding a companion for life should be undertaken only through prayer for God's guidance!

III. ISHMAEL AND ISAAC AT ABRAHAM'S FUNERAL
   (Gen. 25:1-18)

1. *Abraham and Keturah*

Some time after Sarah's death Abraham took another wife, Keturah, who was probably a Canaanite, and she bore him six sons; but they were never given the same rating in the family that Isaac enjoyed. One after another Abraham sent them away to establish their homes elsewhere, laden with gifts; but they were not sharers with the son of promise in the family heritage. Isaac was to be the sole heir of all that Abraham possessed.

2. Ishmael Comes Back

When Abraham died, it had been many years since Ishmael and Hagar had been sent away to wander in the wilderness. It seems now that it must have been necessary for the preservation of God's blessings and promise through Isaac, but it must have been hard for Ishmael to understand. It may be that the Bible does not give us a full account of the circumstances over the years. It would be expecting too much to ask that all the details be given, and some of those omitted items might throw some interesting light on the occasion for sending Ishmael and Hagar away, if we knew them. We do not know all of those circumstances, but the funeral of the father of the faithful gives us a beautiful picture of the family that had passed through so many trying experiences.

Ishmael the wanderer came back to assist Isaac, the meditative son of the covenant, in the funeral of their father. There was no tie drawing him back when Sarah died, but Abraham was his father and evidently he loved him despite the fact that Abraham had refused to make Ishmael a full heir. We have no other record of these two sons coming together in a family meeting. "Abraham gave all that he had unto Isaac" (Gen. 25:5) but Ishmael came back for the funeral. It often occurs that families that have been divided are brought together around a parent's grave. Perhaps the most helpful lesson that we get from Ishmael's life is his willingness to lay aside the grievances of the past and come back to do honor to his noble father. Many another would not have looked above his grievances to recognize the greatness of a loved one, but evidently Ishmael was big enough in character to do that. The two half brothers met here and then parted, probably never to meet again.

IV. BIRTH OF ESAU AND JACOB (Gen. 25:19–28)

While the marriage of Isaac and Rebekah was happy, they were nevertheless grieved because they had no children. For twenty years this condition continued, and often they must have been reminded of Sarah's long barrenness. But it was through prayer that they were united in wedlock, and so now they resorted to prayer with their disappointment.

1. *In Answer to Prayer*

Isaac entreated Jehovah, and his prayer was heard and answered; and Rebekah prayed that she might be guided and sustained. Believing parents today know what it is to walk with God through the valley where children are born, but they walk with the confidence that the loving Father who made them his children will give them their children in health and in happiness. The God of Isaac and Rebekah is the God of every devoted couple today.

2. *Distinctive Natures*

Twins were born to Rebekah, but according to Oriental custom the first-born was as much the chief heir as if there had been years between them. Esau was born first. He was ruddy and hairy and that suggested the name. Jacob grasped his brother's heel, and was given the name that means one who supplants, or one who takes by the heel. These characteristics of the babies were to go with the men throughout life.

Esau became a skilful hunter, roving the fields and delighting in stalking his prey. He frequently came in from a hunt with a fresh kill in the bag, which he would dress carefully and cook over an open fire for his father. It was quite natural that there should develop a tender affection between Isaac and Esau. Was he not his first-born, and would he not inherit the bulk of the family estate? And did he not excel in the very thing that Isaac had always admired but had been too timid to follow boldly?

V. A DECEIVER'S SON (Gen. 26)

Very little is told in the Bible of the life and work of Isaac. He was a quiet home-loving man, devoted to his wife, remaining in the country around Hebron practically all of his life, and following the line of least resistance in most things. In one way it was commendable in him that he was willing to trust his father's servant to go on a long trip to select a wife for him, while he remained at home and prayed, but it was also an indication of lack of initiative. A more vigorous and independent man of forty would have prayed for guidance and then would have gone on the trip himself to look for that wife. Evidently Abraham recognized this fundamental weakness in Isaac, and hence sent the servant instead of his son.

Isaac quite naturally slips into the background when we are studying this part of the Bible, while stronger characters like Abraham, Rebekah, and Jacob grip our attention. He was not a trail blazer, like his pioneer father; but he inherited from Abraham his love for worship and prayer, or perhaps it would be truer to say that it was instilled in him during his early years by his devout mother and father.

1. Telling a Lie About His Wife

Isaac seems also to have inherited his father's weakness for deceiving people. He fell into exactly the same sin that is twice charged to Abraham. Because of a famine he moved to Gerar, having received a revelation from God that it would be better to go there than to move down to Egypt. When the men there asked him about Rebekah he said that she was his sister, for he was afraid that they might kill him to get her. He was a deceiver's son, but with less ground to justify him in his falsehood, for Rebekah was only his cousin, while Sarah was actually Abraham's half sister. But each of them lied in that he did not say that the woman in question was actually his wife, and that was the important point. Do we censure Abraham and Isaac for resorting to falsehood in time of danger? Of course we do, and yet do we not often tell what we like to call "white lies" without as much truth to support us and certainly without so grave a danger threatening us?

2. God's Disapproval Manifested

The point to be noticed about all three of these instances of deception about Sarah and Rebekah is that God did not approve, but manifested his disapproval so positively that the deception was discovered, and then God allowed Abraham and Isaac to prosper in safety and security, as if to rebuke them for their folly in thinking that there could be any protection greater than Jehovah could provide. Falsehood and deception never pay in the business of building a life or constructing a character.

3. Isaac Digs Wells Peacefully

In spite of his moral weakness, and because of God's purpose through him and his descendants, Isaac was allowed to prosper in multiplying his herds and flocks and in gathering an abundant harvest from his planting and in digging wells that his animals might have water. It was in the digging of those wells that he once more exhibited the characteristics of his great father and showed the effects of early home training and left an example that we may well emulate today.

Enemies had stopped up the wells that Abraham had dug, and now Isaac quietly went about the task of renewing them, but more trouble arose. Then he moved on and dug a new

one, and when it was flowing freely hostile herdsmen fought
with his herdsmen for control of it. He might have organized
his servants into an army and fought for that which was his
according to the recognized desert law that a well belongs
to the one who digs it. But, as Abraham had done with Lot,
he yielded the point and moved on to find another. Again
he was successful in finding water, and again there was strife.
One would think that surely he would fight back this time,
but once more he remembered the example of his father
and how God richly blessed him after he gave Lot his
choice of land. Perhaps Isaac also counted the cost. What if
he should win the battle and lose half of his valuable servants? He could dig other wells, and Jehovah would guide
him in the future as he had done in the past. It may be that
it was not God's will that he should settle there. He had
lived by prayer and not by fighting in the past, and he had
been blessed. He would try that path yet again. This time
he dug the well at Rehoboth, and then a little later the one
at Beer-sheba, where he made a covenant with Abimelech
and dwelt in peace and prosperity.

VI. ESTIMATE OF ISAAC

What can be said that will sum up the character study of
Isaac? At least three things:

1. He was like Abraham in prayer and worship. Five times
it is said of Abraham that he built an altar, and once that
act is attributed to Isaac. But many times it is said of the
son that he prayed, or that God spoke to him and revealed
his will to him. We are not surprised at that, for he grew
up in a devout religious environment. Was he not at one
time actually put on the altar as a gift to Jehovah? That must
have made a lasting impression on him, to make him remember always that he belonged to God. That same father, together with the mother who was ever grateful to God for
the gift of a son, frequently led the boy to the altar where

the family worshiped. When he became a man the habit was fixed, and he prayed over every problem.

2. His chief weakness was his tendency to follow the line of least resistance. He was content to send a servant to choose a wife for him, although he was forty years old and should have been quite capable of doing that for himself. He lied about Rebekah when he should have had the courage to tell the truth and trust the Lord to take care of him. In this he was like his father, but he was not like his father in forging ahead and doing things for himself. Abraham sent for a wife for Isaac, but Isaac never did as much for Esau and Jacob. Esau married a Canaanite woman, and Jacob might have done the same if it had not been for the intervention of Rebekah.

3. We must remember Isaac as a peace-loving man. He gained by avoiding war and seeking peace by way of compromise. It is well to remember that "hatred stirreth up strifes: but love covereth all sins" (Prov. 10:12).

Isaac's descendants have learned over and over again what it is to be driven from places of prosperity to establish new homes. Often they have moved under bitter persecution at the hands of those who have envied the Jews their prosperity. But the story repeats itself; when driven from one country they have gone to another and there the Lord has allowed them to prosper. Let us look from the peace-loving Isaac across the centuries to the Prince of peace and covenant with him that we shall live at peace with all men by putting our full trust in God.

FOR CLASS DISCUSSION OR FURTHER STUDY

1. What admirable qualities do you see in Isaac? What weaknesses?
2. Was Isaac great because of his own superior character and personality, or because God had a purpose to carry out through his life? How are believers today like Isaac (Gal. 4:22–31)?

CHAPTER 4

I. EARLY YEARS AT HOME (Gen. 25:29–34)

    1. Differences Between the Twins
    2. Esau Sells His Birthright

II. DECEIVES HIS FATHER AND LEAVES HOME (Gen. 27:1 to 28:9)

    1. Jacob and Rebekah Cheat Esau
    2. Jacob Sent Away

III. REBEKAH

    1. Courteous and Kind
    2. Quick of Discernment
    3. Willing to Sacrifice Herself
    4. Religious
    5. Devoted Mother

IV. JACOB'S FIRST VISIT TO BETHEL (Gen. 28:10–22)

    1. At Abraham's Place of Worship
    2. Jehovah Speaks to Him
    3. Compact with Jehovah

V. WORKS FOR LABAN (Gen. 29–30)

    1. From Bethel to Haran
    2. Serves Laban for Rachel
    3. Deceived by Laban
    4. Receives Rachel
    5. Prospers Through Cunning and Trickery

4

Jacob the Deceiver

Genesis 25:29–34; 27–30

I. EARLY YEARS AT HOME (Gen. 25:29–34)

The relations between the twin brothers, Jacob and Esau, should have been intimate and loving. That is the normal story of twins, for they have so much in common, often look very much alike and usually have similar tastes. But these boys were born struggling together, and that was an omen of the contention of later years.

1. *Differences Between the Twins*

From the very first the twins seemed to be inclined in opposite directions. Esau became a hunter, a man of the fields, living a rough and rugged life, taking things very much as they came. He was never happier than when in the chase after wild game. He would go as fast and as long as his strength would carry him, utterly unmindful of precaution or of provision for the time when he would be exhausted and hungry after the hunt had ended. Then when hunger gripped him he would throw away his future for food with which to satisfy his appetite as quickly as he would risk his life upon the uncertain chances of the chase. He was reckless, impulsive, vengeful, sensuous, and crude. He showed no inclination to rise above material things and cherish spiritual values. He was unconcerned over the spiritual significance of his birthright. Abraham, Isaac, and Jacob built altars of worship, but Esau never did, so far as we know.

Jacob early showed a quieter and more even temperament. He delighted to remain near home or to stay by the flocks in the field not far away. He was the steady, reliable shepherd. As he had time at home to listen to his mother's dreams of the future when the promises of God to Abraham and Isaac would be brought to a larger fulfilment, so he had time with the flocks in the field to make those dreams his own in quiet meditation. He learned to control his appetites and passions, and to cultivate patience in working toward the realization of his ambitions. But he also cultivated cunning and deceit and practiced them with cruel disregard of the welfare of his brother or others who might be involved. He was ready to take advantage of his brother's weakness in time of need and turn it to his own profit.

It may be that Jacob's mother had often told him that before he and Esau were born God indicated to her that he should have the birthright, but that his father had determined that his brother should have it, and so Jacob may have felt that he was fighting with his mother on the side of God against Isaac. But such thoughts never justify resort to the base methods and schemes that Jacob employed. It would have been more in keeping with true religion if he and his mother had waited for the providence of God to accomplish his will in the matter. Here is another instance of the principle that the end does not justify the means.

2. *Esau Sells His Birthright*

When Esau came in from a fruitless hunting expedition, hungry and about to faint from weariness, Jacob was boiling some pottage that gave forth a savory odor. No doubt he had planned the whole thing, having watched his brother often as he came in from his strenuous trips. Some distance from home he planted himself in the field with an abundant supply of well-chosen food, and when he saw Esau coming across the field with no game he stirred up the fire and threw in some more vegetables and waited for hunger, his ally, to present his opportunity.

Esau weakened and fell a victim to Jacob's shrewd scheming and sold him his birthright. Jacob secretly exulted as he saw his brother ravenously devouring the food, but "Esau despised his birthright" (Gen. 25:34). He probably despised the restraints that it would place upon him, and now that his stomach was full he thought that he could take care of himself with his skill as a hunter. After all, he thought, he was not the type for prayer and revelation and divine promises.

II. DECEIVES HIS FATHER AND LEAVES HOME
   (Gen. 27:1 to 28:9)

It was customary among the patriarchs in ancient times for a man to bestow his blessing upon his children just before he died, and it was understood that the blessing pronounced was a promise and a prophecy of prosperity and spiritual welfare. The father approaching death was thought to be in intimate communion with God, and so his blessing was accepted as carrying divine favor. There was little difference between such blessing and the birthright, for the former confirmed the latter and was in agreement with it. The first-born who received the birthright, and therefore the major portion of the inheritance, also received the choice blessing from the father. It was customary for the father, when he felt death approaching, to call his sons around him and bestow his blessings upon them.

1. *Jacob and Rebekah Cheat Esau*

Just as Jacob had watched his chance to cheat his brother out of his birthright, so now he and Rebekah were watchfully awaiting their opportunity to deceive Isaac into giving the favorite blessing to him instead of Esau. When Isaac felt himself growing weaker and decided to proceed with the formality of bestowing his blessing, he called Esau and asked him to prepare a meal for him of his choice wild meat, so that he might enjoy the food and then give his older son his blessing.

Rebekah was listening and as soon as Esau was out of sight she plotted with Jacob how he might deceive his father and cheat his brother. He was basely selfish when he took advantage of Esau to get the promise of the birthright from him, and now he was heartless indeed in taking advantage of his aged father, who was blind and helpless. Of course, his mother took the lead this time, but she was doing it for him in unselfish devotion, while he was doing it for himself in unholy ambition. While his brother was away honestly seeking to please his father, the supplanter was at home working feverishly to cheat him out of his blessing before he returned to defend himself.

There is nothing attractive about Jacob here. Indeed, we are disposed to despise him and wonder why Jehovah accepted such a trickster. But great sin calls for great repentance, which is always matched by sufficient grace for full forgiveness. God did not reject Jacob here, because there was slumbering deep in his heart a spirit that would yet break loose and seek God as vigorously as this other spirit was now following the path of sin. God had to wait a long time for Jacob to find the right attitude of life toward him, but he often has to wait a long time for his servants to seek honestly to do his full will.

The foul scheme was brought to its desired success, and Jacob received the blessing. Scarcely had he left the tent when Esau came in with his game. He carefully prepared a delicious dish and took it to his father with high hopes beating in his heart, for this was his great day. He would inherit the family fortune and enter into the management of his father's affairs. The world seemed glorious in his thoughts; it was as if he stood on some high mountain peak with the full glory of the rising sun in his face, while all the earth beneath him was bathed in light and tinted with rich color. Esau spoke to his father and waited. But the words that came were a crash of thunder and burning lightning to all his dreams. Nothing seemed left to him but dust and ashes. From the valley of despair he cried out, "Hast thou not reserved a blessing for me?" (Gen. 27:36).

The heartbroken father can only wail in anguished reply: "Behold, I have made him thy lord, and all his brethren have I given to him for servants; and with grain and new wine have I sustained him: and what then shall I do for thee, my son?" (Gen. 27:37). The very blessing that Esau had confidently expected to receive had gone to his despised brother. Then, while sobs of anguish wrenched his mighty frame, he cried out pathetically: "Hast thou but one blessing, my father? bless me, even me also, O my father."

2. *Jacob Sent Away*

It is not surprising that Esau hated Jacob with a vengeance now and began to plot his death. But Rebekah, ever alert, discovered the death plot and matched it with another scheme to outwit Esau and save her beloved son. She persuaded Isaac to send Jacob away into Mesopotamia to find a wife among the daughters of her brother, that he might not marry among the heathen women of that land, as Esau had done. Isaac fell in with the plan, and sent Jacob away with the blessing that he had passed on to him from Abraham.

III. REBEKAH

As this is our last glimpse of the mother of the contentious twins, it is a good time to look back over her life and sum up what we learn about her from the account given. These are not single portraits that the writer of Genesis has given us, but family groups. We do not look at the mother without seeing the husband and sons close about her in almost every verse. But it is worthwhile to single out those features that make her character what it is and put her picture off to itself, so that we may learn some lessons from her life.

1. Courteous and Kind

First of all, she was courteous and kind. It seemed quite natural for her to treat Eliezer as she did the first time she saw him. She gladly drew water for him and for his animals— no small undertaking, as camels are noted for their large capacity for water after a desert trip—and she did it with a kindly spirit and genteel manner that must have been a part of her very nature.

2. Quick of Discernment

Rebekah was also quick to size up a situation and sense an opportunity. She recognized in Eliezer a man of some importance before he had revealed his mission. There were many things to indicate his station: the number and character of his camels, his retinue of subordinate servants, his dress, the ring and bracelets that he displayed rather casually, as well as his garments and headdress. All of this she took in with a glance, her womanly intuition telling her more than she had time to reason out. When they were talking a little later in the family circle, and the proposal was passed on to her for decision, she decided at once that she could do no better than accept this offer of marriage. She would move into a family of good station in life, of wealth, and true religion. This same quality of sensing and seizing an opportunity went with her through life, as exhibited in her guidance of Jacob to secure the birthright.

3. Willing to Sacrifice Herself

A third characteristic was her willingness to serve and sacrifice herself for larger interests. When Isaac lied about her, saying that she was his sister instead of his wife, she agreed to the falsehood, although she well knew the danger to herself. She might be taken as a subordinate wife into another man's harem, but she did not hesitate, for she was considering her husband's safety and welfare. When she helped Jacob in his scheming against Esau and Isaac, she knew well that she would have to bear the brunt of the blame for she would have to remain in the tent with Isaac and near Esau while it would always be possible for Jacob to run away, but she did not hesitate.

4. *Religious*

Rebekah was evidently very religious, but of a different type from Isaac. She prayed for strength and guidance and then bestirred herself to bring to pass that which she felt was in accordance with God's plan. She was too ready to rely upon scheming and manipulation and connivance, but she did it with a certain amount of religious conviction. Before we criticize her too severely let us ask ourselves whether we have advanced very far beyond her.

5. *Devoted Mother*

We do well to close the character study of Rebekah by thinking of her as a devoted mother. Before her children were born she prayed for them and through the remainder of her life she mothered them. She favored Jacob, as her husband favored the other boy, and she stooped at times to methods that she should have condemned, but she was always conscientious as a mother. Conscience is not enough, for we must always seek the guidance of the Spirit of God for our consciences; but we must not fail to contrast the customs of Rebekah's day with the Christian civilization of our day.

The unpainted scene in Rebekah's life would picture her in her old age waiting through long and lonely days for

Jacob's return. When she sent him away she thought it would be for only a few days. He could accomplish the journey and get a wife in about the same period of time it took Eliezer to get her and bring her back to Isaac. Esau was the type to cool his temper soon in the zest of a good hunt, and there would be other ways of appeasing him, and so the danger to Jacob would be removed. She waited until the months lengthened into years; the hope in her heart grew faint and her vision became dim, as she sat in her tent door and gazed in the direction of her childhood home, but her beloved son did not return. She was called upon to suffer more than she had anticipated, but that is usually the recompense of deception. She died without the comfort of her favorite son's affectionate embrace.

IV. Jacob's First Visit to Bethel (Gen. 28 : 10–22)

Rebekah and Jacob, a crafty team in scheming, were now separated, and for the first time in his life he faced the world without her shrewd counsel and comforting presence. He traveled about forty miles the first day, and every mile must have added to his burden of suffering and loneliness. True, he had Esau's birthright and his father's blessing, but they were of little comfort to him now. He was leaving his boyhood home, where he had always been protected by his resourceful mother and was facing he knew not what. He may well have thought that he had sacrificed everything to selfish ambition, but whether he regretted it or not he could not turn back. He must swallow that lump in his throat and press on.

1. *At Abraham's Place of Worship*

At eventide the fugitive came to Bethel, his grandfather's shrine. Thoughts of that great man of God now flooded his mind. There is a Jewish tradition that Abraham lived some years after the birth of the twins, and that Jacob was his favorite, as he was Rebekah's, and that the quiet lad and the aged grandfather spent much time together talking over Abraham's earlier years and God's wonderful guidance in his life and the projection of that same guidance through the coming generations of his descendants.

Although the Bible account of the death of Abraham comes before the account of the birth of Jacob, a little figuring reveals that he lived through the first fifteen years of his grandson's life. Abraham was one hundred years old when Isaac was born, and Isaac was sixty years old when the twins were born, which means that Abraham was one hundred sixty years old at that time, and one hundred seventy-five when he died. Thus Jacob was fifteen years old when Abraham died. Many times when Esau was out hunting, Jacob had, perhaps, been at home talking with his grandfather, unconsciously allowing him to mold his thinking and shape his ideals.

These memories haunted Jacob now as he came into the region of Bethel. Abraham had erected an altar here, but how different everything was with him! He was traveling with his beloved Sarah and Lot, under Jehovah's guidance and with divine blessing, while Jacob was fleeing alone. The full meaning of his sin dawned upon Jacob as he compared his life with that of his grandfather, whose memory he revered, and as the shades of night began to fall around him in this strange place, he began to be afraid. He must have thought of Cain, driven away from home because of his sin against his brother and forced to wander in the earth until death released him. He was like Cain, wandering from home and forsaken by God, and not like Abraham. For Jacob, "the sun was set" (Gen. 28:11), symbolically as well as literally. Sin is ever thus; it mars the beauty of home life and destroys the blessing of fellowship with God.

2. *Jehovah Speaks to Him*

With a stone for his pillow, Jacob sought rest. Lonely and tired, heavy of heart, wishing that by some mystic power he might turn time back a few days and right his wrongs, he fell into a fitful sleep. A dream came to him, in which he saw a ladder connecting heaven and earth, with angels ascending and descending on it. Then the voice of God came to him, the God of Abraham and Isaac, the God of the family promise, confirming that promise in him. Jehovah assured the wanderer that the God of Abraham would go with him and keep him, and bring him back to his home land, which God would give to him for a possession, and that God would make his family great.

Jacob awoke, but the dream remained with him. He realized that he was in the presence of God, and he called the place Bethel, which means the house of God. He came there with a tremendous burden of sin, but he was to go away with the consciousness of being forgiven. And Bethel remains a symbol of the place where sinful man may meet holy God and receive cleansing grace, for "where sin abounded, grace did abound more exceedingly" (Rom. 5:20). Jacob uttered an eternal truth when he said, "Surely Jehovah is in this place; and I knew it not" (Gen. 28:16). God is in every place, but sin blinds us to his presence. He was present in Isaac's home back there in Beer-sheba, but Jacob was not in the proper frame of mind to recognize him.

3. *Compact with Jehovah*

Then Jacob sought to enter into a compact with God. He made a vow that if God would go with him and keep him, give him food and clothes, and bring him in peace to his father's house again, then he would always recognize this place as God's house and would give back to God a tenth of all that God should give to him. It was a bargain and so not a very high spiritual elevation for a true worshiper, but it was a lofty pinnacle for Jacob, considering the low level of sin on which he had been living. One does not rebound immediately from sin to the highest spiritual achievement, for that requires growth in grace.

V. WORKS FOR LABAN (Gen. 29-30)

Now Jacob was started in the right direction spiritually. He would slip again into sin, but this Bethel experience would be a staying power in his heart. He traveled like Abraham now, guided by divine wisdom with a definite purpose before him, and no longer like Cain, wandering aimlessly because of his sin. He went with the assurance that God had forgiven what had happened in the past, and would guide and bless him in the future. There were many days yet ahead of him in his journey, but all of them put together were not as long as that first day that he traveled from Beersheba to Bethel with only his sins for company. He traveled now with the conviction that there was a purpose of eternal significance to be accomplished in his life. God always has a plan and purpose in his service for the one whose sins he forgives.

1. *From Bethel to Haran*

Jacob soon came to Haran. At a well he found some shepherds waiting with their flocks until the time for the stone to be rolled away and the sheep watered. It was not uncommon in that country, where water was scarce, to have a great stone before a well to protect it from strangers and marauders and sand storms.

With a light heart Jacob greeted these shepherds as brethren and inquired of them concerning his uncle Laban. Even as he was talking with them, Rachel, a pretty daughter of Laban and therefore Jacob's first cousin, came with her father's sheep which she was tending. At first sight of her,

Jacob's heart leaped within him for joy; he loved her and immediately determined that, by the help of the Lord, he would get her for his wife. With the strength of a new man, his own power seemingly doubled by the consciousness of God's favor and by the thrill of the beauty of this prospective bride, unassisted he rolled away the stone that ordinarily required the work of several men. Then, having watered the sheep, he turned to Rachel and kissed her and wept for joy. In the Orient a man may weep when he is extremely happy without being called effeminate.

Learning that he was Rebekah's son, Rachel took Jacob at once to Laban, and there was great rejoicing as they welcomed him. But soon the enthusiastic greetings subsided and the family settled down to the established routine, with Jacob easily taking a place in the round of work.

2. *Serves Laban for Rachel*

There was some difference between Jacob's visit to the east to get a wife and the errand of the servant Eliezer to get Rebekah. Jacob displayed no costly gifts and was in no hurry to state the purpose of his visit. In fact, it seemed that he came simply to get a job, and he worked for a month without saying anything about wages. Finally Laban asked him to make an agreement as to the wages that he would expect, whereupon Jacob announced that he would work for Laban for seven years, if at the end of that time his uncle would let him have Rachel for his wife. Daughters were regarded as the property of their fathers and were purchased as wives with money or with labor. Eliezer had paid money and jewels and clothes for Rebekah, but Jacob had none of these with him, and he did not impress his relatives with his wealthy station at home; hence, he could hope to win Rachel only by service. The customary period of service for a wife was five to seven years. He showed his estimate of his cousin by offering to work for her the longer period.

3. *Deceived by Laban*

Happy in his love for Rachel and ever cherishing the realization of his Bethel dream as the aim of his life, Jacob worked, and the years flew by as so many days. When he claimed his bride, Laban deceived him and gave him Leah, the older daughter, instead of Rachel. In the marriage ceremony Jacob called Rachel and Leah answered, deceiving him very much as he had deceived Isaac into thinking that he was Esau. Thus did his practice of deception come back upon him like a boomerang.

4. *Receives Rachel*

Laban explained to Jacob that it was not customary to give the younger daughter in marriage before the older. The marriage ceremonies usually lasted a week, and so he told his nephew that he should go ahead with the festivities of the week, and then he would give him Rachel the next week. In return for her, Jacob was to work for Laban another period of seven years. Jacob agreed and got two wives and their handmaids within the course of two weeks, and then began his second seven-year term of service.

5. *Prospers Through Cunning and Trickery*

When the fourteen years had passed, Laban sought to make a new contract with Jacob, for he saw that he had prospered by having him. Jacob recognized his opportunity to gather something for himself, and the old deceiving nature reasserted itself. He had dealt honestly with his uncle these fourteen years and had been deceived at almost every turn. He reasoned that he knew a trick or two himself and could use them to advantage. So for six years longer he worked, employing all the cunning and trickery that he knew to add to the flocks that would be his according to the contract. It was a case of cheat cheating cheat.

Jacob evidently forgot Bethel for the time, set aside his earlier repentance for his sin against Esau and Isaac, and devoted himself fully to accumulating wealth at the expense of his uncle. Ever since his day there have been those who have said that business is simply a matter of murderous competition in which the man who prospers is the man who is the quickest to take advantage of others in a deal. There is much in the business world that is regarded as legal, but cannot be considered right, judged by an adequate standard of ethics. The way Jacob treated Laban was legal, but it was morally wrong.

FOR CLASS DISCUSSION OR FURTHER STUDY

1. Read Romans 9:10–13. What reason do we have for claiming that Rebekah probably believed that through her scheming she was bringing about that which God had ordained? Do you believe her actions were pleasing to God?

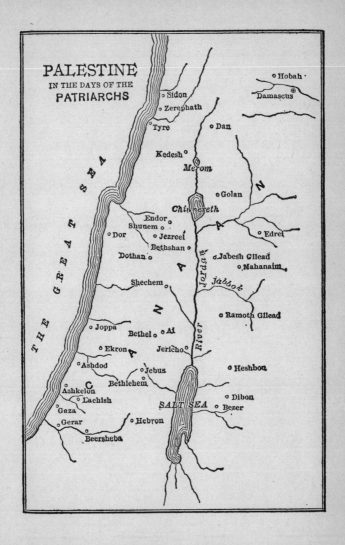

PALESTINE
IN THE DAYS OF THE
PATRIARCHS

THE GREAT SEA

Hobah
Damascus

Sidon
Zerephath
Tyre
Dan
Kedesh
Merom
Golan
Chinnereth
Endor
Shunem
Dor
Jezreel
Bethshan
Dothan
Jabesh Gilead
Mahanaim
Shechem
Jabbok
Jordan

Ramoth Gilead

Joppa
Bethel
Ai
Ekron
Jericho
Ashdod
Jebus
Heshbon
Bethlehem
Ashkelon
Lachish
Dibon
Gaza
SALT SEA
Bezer
Gerar
Hebron
Beersheba

CANAAN
River

CHAPTER 5

5

Israel the Champion of God and Joseph the Dreamer

Genesis 31–37

I. Jacob Leaves Laban (Gen. 31)

Jacob had forgotten the divine purpose in his life in the midst of his unseemly successes, but a condition arose that made him think once again of his home and birthright.

1. *Slips Away with the Help of His Wives*

Laban's sons became jealous of their cousin, and Jacob knew that that meant real danger. So he began to make his plans to leave. He felt that he would have to gather his possessions together and seize an opportunity to slip away unobserved, or have a battle with his uncle. He enlisted the aid of his wives, for their father had violated custom and appropriated their dowery (see Gen. 31:15). The custom was that when a father sold his daughter to a man to be his wife, he gave the money, or a considerable portion of it, to the bride and it became her property, but Laban had kept it all for himself.

It was while Jacob was being disturbed by the thoughts of possible conflict with his uncle that he once again listened to the voice of the God of Bethel. It is often true that in the midst of prosperity God's servants are not sensitive to his guidance, and so he permits temporary disturbances to come to shake them out of their easy content, to enable him to lead them out of something that they think is good to something that God knows is better. Jehovah renewed his promise to Jacob and called upon him to start back to Canaan, for it was there that the call of Abraham was to be worked out in him. As it was necessary for Abraham to leave this country when the call was initiated, so it was necessary for Jacob to leave it when the same call was to be sustained and carried forward.

Jacob had come into this country empty-handed, but he returned rich. Eleven sons and one daughter had been born to him in Paddan-aram, and he had two wives with their handmaids. He also had large flocks of sheep, goats, and many camels and donkeys, as well as many servants and slaves. All of these he gathered together secretly and stole away toward home. He did not want to fight his uncle and cousins, mainly because he was afraid and because he had a guilty conscience over his conduct during the past six years. He had been dishonest with his uncle and therefore he was afraid of him. It was God's will that he should leave this land, but not that he should sneak out like a coward.

2. Overtaken by Laban

As a rebuke to Jacob, and to show that honesty with man and confidence in God is always the wisest and the safest path to follow, Jehovah allowed Laban to overtake the fleeing household. Then when Jacob's plan had failed and the danger that he had feared was about to come into dread reality, God intervened and kept Laban from harming him in any way. When the danger had evidently passed, Jacob became bold and chided his uncle for the way he had treated him, but it was a misplaced boldness. If it had come before he started away it would have indicated strength of character, but here it indicated weakness.

3. *Mizpah*

With their difficulty settled, Jacob and Laban erected a stone memorial, ate a peace meal, and formed a covenant with the Mizpah as the ritual: "Jehovah watch between me and thee, when we are absent one from another" (Gen. 31:49). They agreed that the stones would be a witness that neither would pass over to harm the other.

II. MEETS ESAU AFTER PENIEL (Gen. 32:1 to 33:15)

Jacob had prayed at Bethel, twenty years before, that God would bring him back to his own people in peace, and now the prayer had been answered in his last encounter with Laban. God enabled him to leave in peace, and not in anger and fear as he had fled from his brother and father.

1. *Alarming Report of His Messengers*

But even as Jacob thought of the past, the old fear of his brother came back upon him. How would Esau receive him? He was capable of great anger and terrible vengeance, and Jacob did not regard him as of a forgiving disposition. Indeed, on his own account, Jacob had little reason to expect forgiveness. The more he thought of these things the more he became fearful. Once more he was trusting in himself rather than in Jehovah. Fear gripped him with double force when his messengers returned telling him that Esau was coming to meet him, riding with four hundred men as his bodyguard.

2. *Jacob's Strategy*

What would you have done in such a situation? Would you have prepared for battle, or would you have turned and fled to Laban for protection? There was no time for Jacob to flee with his family for Esau was riding toward him and would easily overtake him as Laban had done. Jacob decided upon two lines of action: He would resort to his best skill and ingenuity in meeting his brother, and he would pray for divine counsel and help. And there he showed his wisdom. There had been times when he had appeared weak and un- promising, but as he grew older he grew stronger, for in critical times he hearkened to the voice of his God. And now in his greatest crisis he showed his best character.

Having divided his herds and servants into two groups, so that there might be some chance of saving half of them, and having sent generous gifts forward to his brother, Jacob sent his wives and children across the Jabbok and remained alone to pray. Looking back over the past twenty years, he remembered his treachery and unfaithfulness, all of which he now confessed to God. Claiming no merit of his own, he rested his plea on the mercy of God, and the promise given at Bethel (Gen. 32:9–12). Can you improve on that approach to prayer? That was the essence of the prayer of the man about whom Jesus told, who went into the Temple, his Bethel, and prayed: "God, be thou merciful to me a sinner" (Luke 18:13). Jesus said that it was a victorious prayer.

3. Prayer and Victory

All night long Jacob wrestled in prayer, determined to wait for Jehovah's blessing. What a struggle it must have been! The cowardly, deceiving nature that dominated him on so many occasions arose mightily within him. With all of his camp on the other side of the brook, there was yet time for him to escape alone. Before Esau could discover his absence he would be able to get a good start, and on a fast camel he could make his getaway. True, he would have to sacrifice his wives and children, as well as his possessions, but that would be better than dying at Esau's hands.

When such thoughts came to Jacob an angel of Jehovah

strove with him to enable him to master them. For many years the two natures had struggled for mastery in him, and often his better self had been defeated in selfishness and cowardice. When he thought of fleeing from his brother and remembered that he was able to succeed after fleeing before, the angel reminded him that it was by the merciful intervention of God that adversity was turned into blessing. With every appearance of the old crafty, deceiving nature, Jehovah's angel struggled with him. He must gain the victory over himself now, once and for all.

Jacob's struggle was typical, was it not? We remember that Paul said: "For I know that in me, that is, in my flesh, dwelleth no good thing: for to will is present with me, but to do that which is good is not. For the good which I would I do not: but the evil which I would not, that I practise" (Rom. 7:18–19).

In the quiet of the dawn the victory came. "Jacob called . . . the place Peniel: for, said he, I have seen God face to face, and my life is preserved" (Gen. 32:30). His name was then changed from Jacob, the deceiver, to Israel, "For," said the angel, "thou hast striven with God and with men, and hast prevailed" (Gen. 32:28). The struggle of more than twenty years came to a glorious victory in this final climactic struggle, through an all-night prayer. Tired but triumphant, Jacob limped from his place of prayer to meet his brother, an old Jacob, but a new man. Come what may, all was well now, for he had settled the matter with his God. Self was no longer on the throne of his life.

4. *Happy Meeting with Esau*

Imagine Jacob's surprise when he saw Esau running forward, unarmed and with no show of fighting, but with outstretched arms in brotherly greeting, calling him by name in tender affection! The clouds of fear were swept aside in the light of forgiveness that shone in Esau's countenance. The love of God which had dwelt in Abraham and Isaac now welled up in the twins' hearts to melt the barriers that sin had built. They had been strangers and enemies, but now they were brothers.

III. SECOND VISIT TO BETHEL (Gen. 33:16 to 35:29)

Esau returned to Edom, where he had taken up his abode, and Jacob went on more slowly because of the children and the cattle, coming after a while to Shechem, where he tarried for a time.

1. *Grievous Sin at Shechem*

The thirty-fourth chapter of Genesis gives us one of the darkest scenes of sin in all the Bible. The sons of Jacob, with their inherited tendency to deceive, attempted to right a grievous wrong with a greater wrong. If there is any one thing that these accounts teach us it is that two wrongs never make a right. The best way to meet sin is not with more sin, but with prayer and trust in God, to be followed by forgiveness.

2. *Call to Bethel*

When the sin of the thirty-fourth chapter was the darkest, God called upon Jacob to go to Bethel and tarry there in prayer and worship. He turned to his family and called upon them to go with him. And when Jacob spoke he was a prophet, for a prophet is one who speaks for God after God has spoken to him. At Bethel they put away their foreign gods and repented and sought forgiveness and guidance. It was a different Jacob who came to Bethel this time. Before, he had been a coward running from his sin, but now he came as the priest of his home and a prophet of God. Before, he had needed sorely to enter God's presence; now his family needed to have him at the altar and to take them with him.

Often it is true that our loved ones and friends need to have us to go to God in prayer and take them with us.

3. *Death of Rachel*

Just beyond Bethel, Rachel died in giving birth to Benjamin, her second son. How fortunate it was that Jacob had heeded God and had gone to Bethel, for he and Rachel were thus prepared for the separation that was soon to come! They had loved each other devotedly from their first meeting. Her death must have been a heavy blow to Jacob, but he was prepared for it now that he had been to Bethel, the house of God. Christian faith is often put to its severest test in the death of loved ones. If we are a long distance and a long time from our Bethel of prayer, faith will be weak, and the world has nothing to take its place; but if we are near our Bethel, we are ready for whatever may come, for God is with us and we are with him.

IV. OLD AGE

Through many trials and vicissitudes Jacob had passed, but at last he had come to a quiet old age. There is no sadder picture than that of a man who comes into the eventide of life confirmed in his sin. All of the sins of the early and vigorous years have become deep-rooted in him. In his reminiscences he lives over again much evil that he has done. But to a man like Jacob, who has triumphed over sin in his prime, and has learned to walk with God in confession and trust, the last years of earthly life are mellowed and sweetened. We are reminded of Browning's lines:

> Grow old along with me!
> The best is yet to be,
> The last of life, for which the first was made
> Our times are in His hand
> Who saith "A whole I planned,
> Youth shows but half; trust God:
> See all, nor be afraid."

1. *Devoted to Joseph*

Sitting in his tent and meditating upon his life, Jacob did not live with his sin, but with memories of God's goodness to him. His life now, however, was not merely a round of meditation; it was in these years that he devoted himself to Joseph, his favorite son. The other sons, with the exception of Benjamin, grew up under his tutelage while he was deceiving Laban, and before Peniel and the second visit to Bethel.

But by the time Joseph was old enough to delight in his father's company, Jacob had won the victory over his sinful nature at Peniel and had taken his family to confession and prayer at Bethel.

When he realized that his family needed to go with him to Bethel for spiritual cleansing, Jacob could not have dreamed what it would mean for the progress of God's purpose through the life of the little lad, Joseph. If we wonder how a son of Jacob was able to withstand the temptations of the court of Pharaoh, we must remember that Joseph grew up under the wise and affectionate counsel of the Jacob of Peniel and Bethel. If no other result came from those years of Jacob's life but the training of Joseph they were tremendously worthwhile.

Here the center of our attention shifts a bit. Jacob begins to fade into the background of the picture, while Joseph comes forward, for it is in his life that the rest of the book of Genesis traces the development of God's purpose to bless the nations of the earth. Our attention is called to Jacob from time to time as we study Joseph, but only incidentally.

2. *Shock of Joseph's Disappearance*

In finishing our life sketch of the patriarch grandson of Abraham, two scenes should be mentioned. The first is the occasion when the tragic report of Joseph's disappearance was brought to him. His years were brightened and blessed with the companionship that he had with Rachel's first son. The love that he had for her, that was his first and greatest love, was somehow sanctified in his love for her two sons, and especially for Joseph. He was enjoying that, after his many unhappy experiences, as one enjoys the quiet beauty of the golden sunset after a storm.

But it sometimes happens that the storm turns in its course and comes back to unleash its fury again, and with driving clouds and wind and rain to stretch a curtain of ominous darkness over the face of the sun. It was even so with Jacob. It seemed that the storm of treachery had passed, and that he and his family had settled down to enjoy the calm of the eventide of his life. But it came back upon him with a fury that was almost fatal to him. When his older sons deceived him and sold his favorite child into slavery, he was reaping a bitter harvest from his own sins of earlier days.

As Jacob had deceived Esau and Isaac and Laban, his sons had learned the same miserable art. They had practiced it on Shechem (Gen. 34), even as they had witnessed their father's success in his deception of their grandfather Laban. It was to be expected that when they became jealous of another member of the family they would not hesitate to employ that same black art against their father. Thus does sin do its deadly work. Never content with doing harm to others for us, it always returns to play tragic havoc with us, and the harm that it does to us is greater than the harm that it does to those whom we try to deceive.

Jacob had won the victory over sin in his own life at Peniel, but he had not checked the growth of the seed that he had unintentionally planted in the lives of his children. He had been forgiven personally, but the full wages of sin were yet to be paid. He had sowed "his wild oats" and the seed had fallen into the hearts of his own sons. And now he must share in the reaping of the harvest. What a different story might have been told if he had had his conversion experience before he cheated Esau out of his birthright! These sons would have grown up under Israel the "Champion of God," instead of under Jacob the deceiver, and they might not have learned to deceive.

3. *Reunion with Joseph in Egypt*

The other scene in Jacob's closing years is the reunion with Joseph and his other sons in Egypt. The storm subsided again, and just in time to allow the last soft rays and glorious flashes of color from the setting sun to fall across the door of Jacob's tent before the day of his life ended and the night of death began. Joseph as a lad did not witness his father plying his craft of wickedness with Laban, but learned from him the ways of righteousness. And now when the harvest came it was one of joy and peace and blessedness, the fruits of righteousness. Once more God's grace had overcome the world's sin where faith could be found, and the result was the glory of God in the happiness of man and the advancement of God's purpose to save the world from sin.

V. JOSEPH THE DREAMER (Gen. 37:1–11)

Looking back a bit we may easily pick up the salient facts about Joseph's life before he was seventeen years old. He was born in Paddan-aram toward the close of the first fourteen years of Jacob's sojourn there, the first son of Rachel.

1. *Early Life*

Joseph was six or seven years of age when his father struggled all night in prayer just before meeting Esau—old enough to be deeply impressed with that crisis and change in his father's life. He was a little older when Jacob took him and the rest of the family to the special consecration service at

Bethel, and it was just a short time after that high experience that he walked through the shadows of deep sorrow in the death of his mother, near Bethlehem. What profound impressions were made upon the child's mind by these experiences, we may well judge by his conduct as a man.

Then followed ten years of intimate and happy association with his father. He became the errand boy of the family, taking messages from Jacob to the older sons and bringing word back from them. There would be days when he would tarry in the fields with his brothers, learning from them many things that a shepherd must know. Soon he was helping them tend the sheep on occasions when he was needed, and perhaps doing many chores near home in connection with caring for his father's cattle and stock.

2. A Tattler

There was so much that was good and commendable in Joseph that we are tempted to put a halo of special sanctity around his head and forget that he was human. But the Bible account always presents the bad along with the good in telling the story of men's lives. There is a suggestion of something not altogether commendable in him in the statement, "And Joseph brought the evil report of them unto their father" (Gen. 37:2). He was a tattler, and there is no one who more quickly incurs the hatred of his brothers than the one who tattles on them. He may have been conscientious in doing it, because of his fondness for his father and his desire to serve him. And he may have exaggerated the reports, because of his desire to please him, without intending to make his tale into a lie or to bring injustice upon his brothers. But when one makes talebearing his business, exaggeration of the reports becomes his chief temptation. Joseph was to learn the truth of the proverb, "Whoso keepeth his mouth and his tongue keepeth his soul from troubles" (Prov. 21:23).

3. *Coat of Many Colors*

Jacob displayed his affection for Joseph by giving him the coat of many colors. It had long flowing sleeves, which prevented one from doing manual labor with it on and therefore suggested that the wearer was of considerable importance and high rank. The richness of texture and color suggested wealth. It may be that the gift of such a coat indicated Jacob's intention to have Joseph receive the birthright, the blessing of the first-born. The brothers would be quick to read such a motive into the gift, after having often observed their father's partiality toward this younger brother. They probably heard also that Joseph had been busy reporting their misdeeds to Jacob, which added to their jealousy of him.

4. *Dreams*

So the brothers were in a hostile frame of mind when Joseph told them of his dreams. The fact that he told them when he should have suspected their enmity indicates that he did not have the deceitful nature that they had inherited from their father. If he had been crafty and cunning in seeking his advantage at the expense of others, he would have told Jacob in private, but he would have left his brothers to learn for themselves after the dreams had been brought to realization. But with naive frankness he told them first, as if he expected them to rejoice with him in whatever good the dreams held in promise for him.

In his first dream he was reaping in the field, and his brothers' sheaves did obeisance to his sheaf. They immediately sensed the interpretation and hated him for having the dream and for taking it seriously enough to tell it, as though he cherished it. In the second dream the sun and moon and eleven stars did obeisance to him. This one he told openly in the family circle, and as a result his brothers hated him the more, and his father rebuked him but kept the saying in his mind, to be recalled and pondered later.

Joseph was an ambitious, enthusiastic, frank, adolescent boy. Selfish, but without deceit, he thought that his loved ones in the family would enter with him into the spirit of the dream. Maybe it was because his father had spoiled him somewhat; certainly it was also because his father had protected him from those experiences that harden a man to the ways of the world. We have known many other adolescent boys to exhibit the same characteristics: too young to know their place in life with any degree of certainty and too inexperienced to know how others would react to their ambitious dreams and yet simply bursting to tell someone. To whom should they speak but loved ones in the intimacy of the family circle? Where all is bright with mutual love and confidence, such dream stories provoke laughter and good-natured teasing, but where there is jealousy already deep-rooted, such stories provoke scowls of scorn and plottings of revenge.

VI. The Sale of a Brother (Gen. 37:11–36)

When one person is jealous there is some danger of trouble, but when several brothers together allow that same evil spirit to grip their hearts and make them hate another brother, the certainty of the danger is thereby heightened. One will urge another with some new evil thought, and another will recall something that the hated brother has said, and so with much talking the fire of hatred is nursed into a mighty flame. How true to human nature! Recall the woman that Burns has told about in his *Tam O'Shanter* who was busy all through the day "nursing her wrath to keep it warm." So many people nurse their grievances, seeming to derive some sort of fiendish delight from so doing. Joseph's brothers were much more dangerous together than they were alone, because they sympathized with one another too much in their imagined trouble and exaggerated their common fear.

When Jacob sent Joseph on an errand to his brothers there was no suspicion in the lad's mind. He probably started out with his dreams for his thoughts and lived with them as he trudged along the way. What if his brothers and father did not believe them as he did? They might come true some day, and then they would see that he was not just an idle dreamer. With this splendid coat, and his father believing in him as he evidently did, he would be ready to make a start soon. Perhaps his father would let him have a flock and a few servants to himself. And how he would work to prove his metal! With Jehovah's favor upon him he would grow wealthy and powerful.

As he was coming across the fields toward them near Dothan, the brothers recognized him and began to plot against him. They had talked about him so much that they were ready to do almost anything to get rid of him. A few days before they might have been content with whipping him and sending him home, but now that they had worked up their feelings with so much talking, they were desperate. They were about to agree to kill him when Reuben intervened and suggested that they put Joseph in a deep pit. It was his intention to come back later and deliver Joseph from the pit and restore him to their father.

But as the brothers were eating, another opportunity presented itself in the appearance of some Ishmaelite tradesmen on the caravan route to Egypt. Judah suggested that they sell Joseph as a slave, which they did. They sold their own brother to some of their cousins, for these Ishmaelites were descendants of the half brother of their grandfather.

The coat of many colors was dipped in the blood of a goat and taken to Jacob, with the implied suggestion that a wild beast had devoured him. The blow seemed more than the old patriarch could bear. He felt that he surely would die of grief, for Joseph was the idol of his heart and the one in whom he had hoped that the promise of God at Bethel would be sustained and fulfilled. There was no other son of like temperament to take his place. The older ones were rough like Esau, and Benjamin was but a child of nine or ten. All Jacob's fond hopes and cherished dreams crashed around him. His sons in mock sympathy tried to console him, but he would not be comforted.

FOR CLASS DISCUSSION OR FURTHER STUDY

1. As you consider the whole life of Jacob, what is your estimate of his character? Why could God use such a man?
2. Over twenty-five times in the Bible God calls himself "the God of Jacob" or calls Jacob "my servant." Show why Jacob is a good demonstration of what the power of God can do in changing a human being.
3. What is the meaning of Malachi 1 : 2–3 and Romans 9 : 13?

CHAPTER 6

I. POTIPHAR'S SERVANT (Gen. 39:1–20)
1. Tested
2. Promoted
3. Tempted
4. Unjustly Punished

II. THE JAILER'S SERVANT (Gen. 39:21 to 40:23)
1. Faithful in Prison
2. Trusted Friend of Jailer and Prisoners
3. Interpreter of Dreams

III. PHARAOH'S SERVANT (Gen. 41:1–44)
1. Pharaoh Dreams
2. The Butler Remembers
3. Joseph Interprets Pharaoh's Dreams

IV. THE PEOPLE'S SERVANT (Gen. 41:45–57)

V. HIS BROTHERS' SERVANT (Gen. 42:1 to 45:20)
1. Brothers Seek Help
2. Taken for Spies
3. Simeon Kept as a Hostage
4. Return with Benjamin
5. The Test of the Cup
6. Judah's Plea

VI. GOD'S SERVANT (Gen. 45:21 to 50:26)
1. Jacob and Joseph Reunited
2. The Children of Israel Settle in Goshen

6

Joseph the Servant of God

Genesis 39 to 50

IT WOULD SEEM that it was necessary for Joseph to get away
from home. If his brothers had been kind and spiritual in
their treatment of him, he might have grown there into the
servant that God intended that he should be. But they
were not of that type and so it was best for him to get away.
God could guide him in Egypt better than he could in his
home. Once again God was overruling evil for good. "And
we know that to them that love God all things work together
for good, even to them that are called according to his purpose" (Rom. 8:28).

I. POTIPHAR'S SERVANT (Gen. 39:1–20)

When the Ishmaelites arrived in Egypt, Potiphar, the
captain of Pharaoh's guard, bought Joseph to serve as a
slave in his house. "And Jehovah was with Joseph, and he
was a prosperous man" (Gen. 39:2). There is the secret
of all of his successes in the land of his forced adoption.

1. Tested

It was a considerable depression in Joseph's ambitions
when he was reduced from the joyous exulting at home, as
he wore his handsome coat, to the humble routine of a house
slave, but God was with him. The ambitious lad was beginning to learn the lesson that every servant of God must

75

master: to walk with God humbly and gratefully in all circumstances.

2. *Promoted*

As Joseph prospered in his work, his master observed him, placed confidence in him, and then promoted him. As he continued to serve well, Potiphar's confidence grew until he made Joseph the custodian and overseer of all his material possessions and allowed him to come and go in his home with the freedom of a member of the family, but it was understood that a rigid prohibition was put upon him where Potiphar's wife was involved. Of course, he was not to touch her. He needed not to be told about that, for he came from a home where the relations between husband and wife were surrounded with a certain amount of sanctity. Nevertheless, the temptation came.

3. *Tempted*

Joseph in his prosperity had become a handsome man, and now his master's wife became lustfully interested in him and attempted to seduce him. Whether or not there was a struggle within Joseph before he was able to resist the temptation the account does not tell us, but we may rest assured that there was. The temptation did not come to him unexpectedly, but grew gradually from day to day, and he reasoned what he would do if she should approach him. And he did a noble thing: he looked upon the temptation in the light of his relation to Potiphar, his true neighbor, and in the light of his relation to God. If he yielded to such a temptation he would violate all the trust that his master had reposed in him, and he would be going contrary to all the religious training that he had received at home and would commit a heinous sin against Jehovah his God and the God of his father.

It is no wonder that Joseph was able to resist the temptation. He studied it beforehand and saw it as sin in its social and religious relations. All of us would be cleaner and better if we would follow his example. Multitudes of sins are committed by people who rush headlong into temptation without considering its certain consequences, or its influence upon their relationship to their fellow man and to God. Joseph was ready when the temptation came because he had prepared against that time with prayer to God and honest thought about his neighbor.

4. *Unjustly Punished*

Joseph escaped the temptation unscathed by sin, but the evil scheming of the sinful woman brought suffering upon him. And that was to be expected, for that is the way sin works. When the tempter fails to lead an innocent person into sin, then all the fury of hell is turned loose to make the innocent suffer. Young people should remember that when they begin following evil companions. The story of Joseph gives us a lesson about sin that is true in every generation.

II. The Jailer's Servant (Gen. 39:21 to 40:23)

When Joseph was unjustly sent to prison there is no indication that he sulked in bitterness over his fate. So far as we know, he did not even protest to Potiphar, but trusted in Jehovah that everything would work out right. He was there because of an evil report that was told about him. One wonders if he did not recall how he had carried evil reports to his father about his brothers. Sin was acting like a boomerang with him, as it had done in Jacob's experience. But Joseph was learning his lesson early. He was more responsive to chastening than was Jacob, and so God was able to make a righteous servant of him in a shorter period of time. When it seemed that God had overlooked him, "the word of the Lord tried him" (Psalm 105:19).

1. *Faithful in Prison*

No longer a mere lad, but now a full-grown man with a strong faith in God, and with a determination to meet his fellow man on the ground of that faith, Joseph went about his new duties in the jail with the same confidence, courage, and cheerfulness that he had exhibited when he prospered in Potiphar's house. What better indication of strength of character could be given? How often it is true that men who were bold in their confidence during prosperity become hopelessly morose and bitter in adversity and depression!

In the years following the depression of 1929, we heard of hundreds of wealthy men committing suicide when they saw their fortunes slipping through their fingers. Joseph was made of different timber, and he had been trained by Jacob after Peniel. In prison he prayed much and made himself happy in humble service. Can we adjust ourselves after a social and financial disruption with as much grace and poise? Paul said, "For I have learned, in whatsoever state I am, therein to be content" (Phil 4:11). That is a real test of religion.

2. *Trusted Friend of Jailer and Prisoners*

Joseph was as trustworthy in prison as he was in places of wealth. The saying of Jesus, "He that is faithful in a very little is faithful also in much" (Luke 16:10), works both ways. He that is trustworthy in great matters is also trustworthy in little things. The jailer soon found that Joseph could be trusted, and so he put him in charge of the other prisoners. And, more remarkable still, the prisoners felt that they could put their confidence and trust in him. He was superior to them in every way, and yet he did not impress them that he thought as much, but, rather, he was good to them and loved them and they responded to his kindness.

They turned to him with their problems, having more confidence in his wisdom and integrity that they had in the professional interpreters and "fortunetellers" of their day.

3. *Interpreter of Dreams*

When the baker and the butler told Joseph their dreams and asked him to tell the meaning, he replied in characteristic manner: "Do not interpretations belong to God? tell it me, I pray you" (Gen. 40:8). That answer showed the habit of prayer and confidence in God, rather than conceit and self-reliance. Joseph had confidence in himself only as the servant of God. If they would tell him their problem, he would ask God for the answer and then give it to them. They were not accustomed to hearing that from the professional interpreters. But then this man was different. Being a dreamer who prayed over his dreams, he was ready to interpret theirs.

The butler's dream meant that he would, within three days, be restored to his position in Pharaoh's service. Here was an opportunity not to be overlooked, far better than a friendly emissary to Potiphar. If Joseph could get a word of friendly recommendation to Pharaoh, his misfortune of being sent to prison would turn out to be a blessing in disguise. He could not know what God had in store for him, to be brought about through this favorable contact, but he was alert to seize an opportunity to get out of his present predicament. His deliverance was to come, though not at once, and it was to be brought to him from God through humble service and in answer to prayer.

Joseph also unraveled the mystery of the baker's dream. But it did not have a happy conclusion. Events soon proved that Joseph was right in his interpretations, but the butler forgot his promise. Joseph's lesson in discipline was not quite complete, and the time was not ripe for him to come into Pharaoh's court. But as Joseph kept faithful and patient in prayer, God brought his providential purpose to a happy culmination in the life of his servant.

III. PHARAOH'S SERVANT (Gen. 41 : 1–44)

For two long and monotonous years after the butler left him Joseph continued to serve in the prison. He must have been sorely tempted to lose all faith in man, if not in God. The friend whom he had helped had forgotten to return the kindness, when all that he needed to do was to speak a word for his benefactor. But years that seem long and dreary while they are passing appear as but a moment when we look back upon them from the vantage point of prosperity and happiness.

1. *Pharaoh Dreams*

Pharaoh had two dreams that disturbed him much, for he felt that they must portend something about the days ahead of him that he should know. The wise men were called in, but his dreams were too much for them. Then the butler awoke from his two years of unkind forgetfulness of his fellow prisoner. He had left the prison with the good intention of returning Joseph's kindness, but when adversity left off and prosperity and ease began, he forgot the one who helped him in the day of his need.

We should not take the butler's oversight so seriously if his unkindness had ceased with him, but his like have been legion in every generation since, and his sin runs so true to unregenerate human nature that we must put ourselves on guard lest we too become the victim of it.

2. *The Butler Remembers*

But the butler woke up! Give him credit for finally coming to his senses. Joseph was summoned from the prison and presented to Pharaoh. He was older for his years in prison, but not harder. So many men come out of hardship hardened and cynical, but Joseph came out chastened and consecrated, more willing than ever to seek divine guidance in service. When Pharaoh flattered him with the report that he had heard of his ability to interpret dreams, he answered, "It is not in me: God will give Pharaoh an answer of peace" (Gen. 41 : 16). He was still the man of prayer, waiting for God to lead him. And he did not miss an opportunity to witness for Jehovah. In that respect he was greater than his great-grandfather, Abraham, who had been afraid to acknowledge his faith in Jehovah in the land of Egypt. We often fail to use similar opportunities to teach the importance of prayer. The Christian should live by prayer and diligently seek to in-fluence others so to live. We may rest assured that God is as ready to guide our friends through us in answer to prayer as he was to guide Pharaoh through Joseph in answer to prayer.

3. Joseph Interprets Pharaoh's Dreams

Joseph told Pharaoh that his dreams meant that seven years of famine would follow seven years of plenty. Joseph then suggested a plan whereby provision could be made in the years of plenty for the famine. That was an answer to prayer, too, though indirect. When he prayed for guidance his native ability was quickened, his judgment was better, his thinking was clearer. Pharaoh liked the suggestion, and said to his court, "Can we find such a one as this, a man in whom the spirit of God is?" (Gen. 41 : 38). Joseph had said that a man "discreet and wise" should be chosen for the task, and now Pharaoh said to him, "There is none so discreet and wise as thou." Did Joseph have himself in mind when he made the suggestion? Perhaps, but he did not recom-mend himself. He waited for others to discover his worth. His times were "in his hand who saith 'A whole I planned.'" He did not seek preferment, but he was ready to serve, and God opened the way for larger service.

IV. THE PEOPLE'S SERVANT (Gen. 41:45-57)

When Pharaoh put him in the place of great authority and told him to follow his own judgment in working out his plans, Joseph looked upon his position as an appointment to serve the people. It was neither the pinnacle of personal glory, nor a step to something higher, but a call to service that was sufficient in itself. He showed no inclination to usurp authority or to make it count for his own profit. When he was the servant of all the people he was as simple in his manner and as profound in his sincerity as when he served his fellow prisoners.

Joseph's wisdom was vindicated in the success that he had in organizing the country in preparation for the days when relief would be needed. He had storehouses provided in central places, and a portion of every crop was laid by for future use. Before the days of plenty came to an end, all the storage places were filled to capacity.

Joseph married and settled in his own home, and two sons were born to him, Manasseh and Ephraim. But he must have thought often of his father and brothers. He had never heard how his father reacted to the shock of his sudden disappearance. He often wondered if he were still alive. And the brothers! Were they still envious of him? Perhaps he thought of going back for a visit, but it would not be pleasant if they still hated him, and anyway he was busy saving grain against the famine that was sure to come. O yes, the famine! That would bring some of his family down to Egypt in search of food, for Palestine was frequently visited by droughts, at which time the people usually looked to Egypt for help. That was what had brought Abraham and Sarah into this land many years before. The famine that was coming would bring many Palestinians down to this land, and his brothers might be among them.

V. His Brothers' Servant (Gen. 42:1 to 45:20)

Jewish tradition has it that Joseph followed this intimation of his own reasoning by stationing guards on all the main roads, with instructions to report the names of all Palestinian travelers in the land.

1. Brothers Seek Help

In the second year of the famine the brothers came. They were coming for help into the land whither they had sold Joseph as a slave twenty-one years before. Through all these years Jacob had refused to be comforted by them. They had thought that he would get over his sorrow shortly and they would all forget their "smart" little brother. But when people commit crime they never understand how deep are the furrows they plow in the hearts of those they wrong. Because Jacob had grieved so deeply they had grieved too. Perhaps they had often wished that they might have Joseph back with them. Jacob would be so glad to see him again, and they could forget his youthful dreams.

Now as they journeyed toward Egypt, we can almost hear Reuben saying to his brothers that this may be their opportunity to right their great wrong. In fact, he may have told them that perhaps God had sent the famine upon them to take them down into Egypt so that they might find Joseph and buy him back out of slavery.

2. Taken for Spies

As they talked about it, a plan took shape in their minds. They would scatter throughout the land and look in the places where slaves were most likely to be found, and after they had found Joseph they would buy grain and return joyously to Jacob. This they did, but they were being watched by Joseph's servants who reported that they must be spies.

When they had failed to find their brother, so goes the Jewish tradition filling in the Scripture account, and the time had grown late, they met at a central granary and applied for a purchase.

Joseph had them brought into his presence. He would fain have thrown himself upon their necks and kissed them as his own brothers, but he did not yet know their attitude toward him. He must try them and see whether they would receive him in brotherly affection. In assumed gruffness he accused them of spying upon the land and had them thrust into prison for three days. Were they not the cause of his spending more than two years in prison? But this was no scheme of vengeance. He was seeking to know the true condition of their hearts before he revealed himself to them.

3. *Simeon Kept as a Hostage*

Having bound Simeon as a hostage, to make sure that they would return with Benjamin, Joseph sent them away with bountiful provisions and with each man's money in his sack. Simeon was the second oldest. Joseph's brothers must have been startled when he showed such strangely accurate knowledge of them. Reuben was the oldest, and therefore the logical one to be detained, but it was he who had attempted to save Joseph when his brothers plotted to kill him as a lad of seventeen.

4. *Return with Benjamin*

With great difficulty the brothers persuaded Jacob to let Benjamin accompany them on their next trip to Egypt. Reuben and Judah promised to stand surety for him and protect him with their lives. With a heavy heart Jacob consented, loading them with gifts and money to take to the ruler, and praying, "God Almighty give you mercy before the man" (Gen. 43:14). That prayer was answered, and "the man" whom he feared turned out to be the son whom he loved.

The dramatic story of Joseph's treatment of his brothers is not excelled in all literature. No matter how familiar we may be with it, it grips us anew with every fresh reading. When the brothers returned with Benjamin, Joseph provided a private banquet for them in his home. This overwhelmed them and they became suspicious. It is not uncommon among certain Orientals to entertain an enemy at a feast just before wreaking vengeance upon him, and this is what they expected, for their guilty consciences smote them. But they presented their gifts to Joseph, having returned the money from their sacks to the chief servant with an apologetic explanation, "and bowed down themselves to him to the earth" (Gen. 43:26).

Thus was Joseph's childhood dream fulfilled, but he took no joy in the thought that at last he had his brothers bowing before him. On the contrary, when he looked upon them and saw Benjamin, his heart overflowed, and he had to rush out of the room to avoid bursting into tears before them. After his first outburst he was able to control his emotions, and they went on with the feast.

5. *The Test of the Cup*

Joseph had forgiven his brethren, and they had lost their envious hatred for their younger brother and were filled with a genuine desire to find him and restore him to their father. Their hearts were ready for the happy reunion, but Joseph did not know their hearts, and they did not recognize him. It required a testing time for the brothers to reveal their deeper emotions to each other. That came when they started home, laden with provisions.

Joseph's cup had been put purposely in Benjamin's sack, to determine whether the other brothers still had the same evil spirit that they had shown when they sold Joseph into slavery. If they allowed him to keep Benjamin as a slave when the cup was found in the sack, he would know that their hearts had not undergone a change. If they were different men now, they would try to save their younger brother. We must remember that Joseph and Benjamin were full brothers, and the others were their half brothers. It was a perfectly planned test, and the result exceeded Joseph's fondest dream.

6. *Judah's Plea*

Judah's plea will forever remain a classic. Turn to it now and read it through (Gen. 44:18–34). His plea was not primarily for his younger brother, but for his aged father. He begged Joseph to let him become his slave in Benjamin's place and thus save his father from killing grief. It was enough. Joseph knew now that his brothers were of a different spirit. The moving appeal on behalf of his father was more than he could bear. He must reveal himself to them and talk more intimately with them about Jacob.

Joseph not only forgave their sin against him, but he sought to lead them to see that God had a good purpose in it all. They needed to see the greater good accomplished through God's sovereign mercy and to forget the evil of the past. He was their brother, but God had put him in a position where he could serve them in their time of need. They must hasten back to Jacob and bring him and all their families and flocks down to Egypt, where they would live on the bounty of the land. They had sold Joseph to be a slave, but God had raised him up to be a savior, and he rejoiced in being able to serve them, for he loved them.

VI. GOD'S SERVANT (Gen. 45:21 to 50:26)

Can you imagine the scene when the brothers returned to their father? Jacob was sitting out in front of his tent looking off toward the south. His servant, watching by his side, saw a cloud of dust on the horizon. He told his master and together they watched it with growing interest. The servant remarked that it was no ordinary train that was coming. Then he noticed wagons, and he observed that they were Egyptian. In fact, he saw the emblem of Pharaoh on them. As the old patriarch heard this, his heart sank within him, for he was sure that Pharaoh had made prisoners of his sons and sent for him to make him a prisoner also.

1. Jacob and Joseph Reunited

As Jacob groaned over this added sorrow that he felt certain was coming upon him, the sons came racing forward on their camels, shouting as they came: "Joseph is yet alive! He is the man whom we feared! He rules over all the land of Egypt, second only to Pharaoh! You are to come with us, and we are all to move down there and live with him!" Did one ever make such a rapid change as did Jacob, from the depths of despair to the heights of inexpressible joy? He was not only to have his son restored to him, but he was to live with him through the remainder of his life.

2. The Children of Israel Settle in Goshen

It was a great joy to the family, but the greater fact about it is that God was carrying forward his purpose in the covenant established with Abraham. Foreseeing the famine years before it came, God prepared the way through Joseph to bring Israel's family into Egypt to preserve them and make a mighty people of them, so that they might come back into the land promised to Abraham and possess it. Joseph's patience in undergoing hardship and his loyalty to righteousness made him a worthy servant of God.

Joseph had become a member of Pharaoh's court, adopting the manner and dress of the Egyptians, and moving with ease in their society. Nevertheless, he did not deny that he was a Hebrew, and when his father and brothers came he presented them to the ruler of all the land. The Egyptians looked with scorn upon shepherds, and of this Joseph warned his brothers, but he was proud to own them as his own kin. He was never greater than in this scene. He was too big in heart to fear for his position if the king should know of the humble station of his family. Pharaoh, through his regard for Joseph, accepted gladly the blessing that Jacob bestowed.

The Genesis account closes with the children of Israel settled in the land of Goshen. There Jacob died, and there Joseph also ended his earthly career many years later.

FOR CLASS DISCUSSION OR FURTHER STUDY

1. What principle of resisting sin is illustrated in Joseph's experience at Potiphar's house?
2. What previous experiences in Joseph's life helped to prepare him to serve in the high governmental position in Egypt?
3. Cite instances from the story of Joseph which illustrate Romans 8:28.
4. Find in Genesis 50:26 an evidence of the faith of the Hebrews that they would be delivered from Egypt. How long did they keep the body of Joseph before burial (Josh. 24:32)?

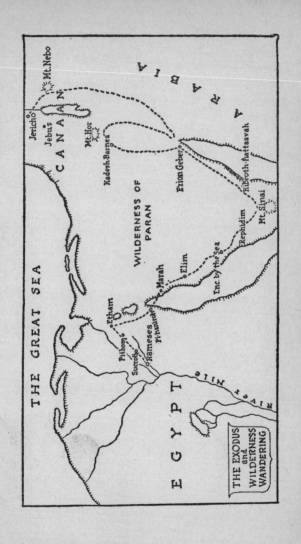

THE EXODUS
and
WILDERNESS
WANDERING

CHAPTER 7

I. BENEFITS DERIVED FROM THE BONDAGE (Ex. 1:1–7)

II. BIRTH AND CHILDHOOD OF MOSES (Ex. 1:8 to 2:10)
  1. Israelites Oppressed by Pharaoh
  2. Moses Born into a Family of Faith
  3. Adopted by the Princess
  4. Nursed by Jochebed
  5. Trained in the Court of Pharaoh

III. FIRST ATTEMPT TO DELIVER HIS PEOPLE (Ex. 2:11–22)
  1. Kills an Egyptian
  2. Flees to Midian

IV. CALL AND COMMISSION (Ex. 2:23 to 4:31)
  1. Meditations in Midian
  2. Called at the Burning Bush
  3. Aaron Called to Help

V. CONTEST WITH PHARAOH (Ex. 5–10)
  1. The Issue
  2. Rods and Snakes
  3. Nine Plagues

VI. THE PASSOVER (Ex. 11:1 to 13:16)
  1. The People Prepared
  2. The Passover
  3. Deliverance

7

Moses the Deliverer

Exodus 1:1 to 13:16

OUR ACCOUNT skips a period of many years, in which the children of Israel grew from a family group of about seventy to a multitude of between one and two million souls. Before we take up the story with Moses we may notice briefly some of the effects of that long and trying sojourn in the land of the Pharaohs.

I. BENEFITS DERIVED FROM THE BONDAGE (Ex. 1:1–7)

Because opposition arose, the Israelites were welded into a mighty union, and in union there is strength. In Palestine they would have wandered about and married into other national groups and thus dissipated their national heritage, but in Egypt they were forced to seek comfort and companionship in their own camps, for the Egyptians despised them as menial servants and treated them roughly. That has been a characteristic experience with the Israelites even to the present. When they have been abused they have been solidified into a unity that has given them strength, but when conditions have been easy for them and they have received kind treatment, they have drifted away from their clannishness and have been assimilated in some measure with other national groups.

They also derived much cultural benefit from their close contacts with the Egyptians. The Israelites were slaves, and as such were thrown into a very intimate relation with their masters. They learned much from the Egyptians and cherished it, but, being slaves, they were not able to throw off their nationality and become Egyptians and so were forced to hold on to their religion and other treasures of their heritage, while at the same time acquiring as much as they could from the natives of their adopted country. It was an important part of the wise providence of God for his chosen people.

They must have learned something of military tactics, for the Egyptians at that time were good soldiers. Being forced to settle in one place and work out their livelihood there, they had to become masters of agriculture, as well as of the arts of weaving and making furniture. They learned music also and discovered their own native ability to compose songs and sing in unison the inspiring themes of their religion. All these things were to help them immeasurably later when God led them out to become a great nation.

As the last of the Genesis account was closed with the story of Joseph, so this new period opens with a study of the life of Moses. He was a character of a new type. He has been called Moses the practical, in distinction from the earlier leaders who were idealists. He was called the meekest man of all the earth (Num. 12:3), a man of great faith (Heb. 11:24-29), and a prophet of the type of Christ (Deut. 18:15-19; Acts 3:22-26). Before you go further with the story here, turn to your Bible and read Hebrews 11:23-29.

II. BIRTH AND CHILDHOOD OF MOSES (Ex. 1:8 to 2:10)

When the Pharaoh "who knew not Joseph" (Ex. 1:8) came to the throne, the Israelites began to suffer severe hardships. They were treated as slaves, driven under whips to perform their tasks, and then given no just part in the fruit of their labor. Because they worked hard and were guided in their religion to be temperate and frugal, rather than self-indulgent and profligate, they were strong and much to be feared if they should ever become organized under hostile leadership.

1. Israelites Oppressed by Pharaoh

Being ever alert to possible rebellion or invasion, Pharaoh concluded that it would be wise strategy to discipline the Israelites and control them while he had the opportunity and before they could cause trouble.

It was in line with this policy that the order was sent out that the Israelites should be afflicted grievously as they performed their tasks and later that the male babies born to the Hebrew women should be killed. But the Egyptians were not able to do all the evil that they purposed in their hearts, for God was with his chosen people and protected them.

2. Moses Born into a Family of Faith

Amram, a member of the tribe of Levi, married a cousin from the same tribe, whose name was Jochebed, and to them were born three children: Miriam, Aaron, and Moses. These children, who were to figure so prominently in the history of their people, were given a good start in life by having a great mother and a good father. The name Jochebed means "Jehovah-thy-glory," which signified the spirit of her life. In the midst of affliction she rejoiced that she could trust in God, and she determined to serve him at all cost. In Hebrews 11:23 it is said, "By faith Moses, when he was born, was hid three months by his parents, because they saw he was a goodly child; and they were not afraid of the king's commandment." Moses became a man of faith because his mother and father lived by faith, because his early life was spent in a home of faith.

You remember the scene so beautifully depicted by Burns in his poem, *The Cotter's Saturday Night,* where the parents gather their children around them as they seek guidance in the Word of God and in prayer. The poet quite truly concludes, "From scenes like these old Scotia's grandeur springs." And it was from such a home as Amram and Jochebed provided that Israel's glory as a nation was to spring. The strength of a nation will always be in the parents and homes where the children get their start in life.

3. *Adopted by the Princess*

The wise and agile mother was able to hide the child away for three months, and then the time came when a bold step must be taken. Everything must be risked on faith in God for the welfare of the child. What risk she took, we fail to appreciate. What if Pharaoh's daughter had failed to take a kindly interest in the child, but had turned him over to the guards? Not only would the child have been destroyed, but in all probability the parents would have been killed also. But she had faith, and that turned her risk into a glorious venture that she knew would somehow turn out well.

When the baby-filled basket was placed where the daughter of Pharaoh usually bathed, the sister was there to watch for her opportunity. Faith always seeks the wisest possible plan and never takes an unnecessary risk. When the child was discovered Miriam was ready with the suggestion about a nurse and was commanded to secure one.

4. *Nursed by Jochebed*

Jochebed was called and employed to care for her son, with wages promised. The plan worked and God richly rewarded her faith; she not only saved her son but received material compensation in addition. She was not trying to make money, but to save her child. God gave the child to her and also a measure of material blessings. Jesus promised the same principle when he said, "Seek ye first his kingdom, and his righteousness; and all these things shall be added unto you" (Matt. 6:33).

"And the woman took the child, and nursed it. And the child grew, and she brought him unto Pharaoh's daughter, and he became her son" (Ex. 2:9-10). What a story of faith! Jochebed gave her best to the child in training him in his tender years, and then when he was the sweetest and the dearest to her she gave him up to become the son of another, because it was God's will and for the highest good of the child. In Pharaoh's court he would have the best advantages in all the land, and perhaps in all the world. He would receive education and culture there that he could not possibly get elsewhere. She stifled her sobs, controlled her emotions, and sacrificed herself for her child's welfare. That is what mothers are for. Their children are given to them to serve God and the world and not to indulge their selfish sentiments. The true mother is happiest when she is able to present her children to God for service.

It is thoroughly likely that Jochebed continued to nurse him after she presented him to Pharaoh's daughter. He was with his adopted mother only a short while every day and with his teachers a longer period, and then his nurse-mother had the privilege of putting him to bed, attending to his clothes, and seeing that he was presentable when the princess called for him. Fading more and more into the background, the mother was comforted as she saw her son receive the highest privileges in the land. In the minutes that he was with her, as she changed his clothes and bathed him, or tucked him in bed, she would tell him that all of these blessings were coming to him in answer to her prayers and to prepare him for a great life of service that Jehovah God must have in view for him. She must have often said to him: "It may be that you will be the chosen deliverer of our people, for God promised through Joseph that he would not leave us in this land. There must come a deliverer some time and I am praying that you, my son, may be the one."

5. *Trained in the Court of Pharaoh*

Moses' training in those early years was of tremendous importance, although little is said of it. He got his early religious training at home and never departed from it. All that he learned at school was built upon the foundation of the principles of faith in God that he learned at his mother's knee and at the family altar, and that is as it should be. In the best schools of Egypt he was an apt pupil, grasping readily what the wisest teachers had to impart. And in the king's palace he imbibed the best culture that the world had to offer. He "was instructed in all the wisdom of the Egyptians; and he was mighty in his words and works" (Acts 7:22).

III. FIRST ATTEMPT TO DELIVER HIS PEOPLE (Ex. 2:11-22)

The training that Moses received under his mother's tutelage while he was becoming expert in the wisdom of the world, did not go for naught. He mastered the sciences of his day, but he also remembered his mother's religion and her prayers that he might be his people's deliverer. He became an Egyptian in manner and speech, but he remained an Israelite at heart.

1. *Kills an Egyptian*

One day Moses took it upon himself to visit his people and look for an opportunity to help them. He was getting well along toward forty years of age, in the prime of life, strong and alert and well educated. If God wanted him to deliver Israel, he mused, he must be getting at it. He would never accomplish it by sitting around the court. He must get out where his people were and show them what he meant to do. We can well imagine that he was meditating thus as he walked along.

He did not have to go far to find a case that called for

a deliverer. Seeing a fellow Hebrew being abused by an Egyptian foreman, "he looked this way and that way, and when he saw that there was no man, he smote the Egyptian, and hid him in the sand" (Ex. 2:12). Then he returned to his room in Pharaoh's palace, feeling confident that he had made a good beginning in this business of delivering. That Israelite would tell his family, and the word would spread in secret whisperings that Jehovah had raised up another Joseph in the court of Pharaoh, who would surely deliver them soon from their sad plight.

But if Moses found satisfaction in such musing it was short-lived, for the second day when he went out to strengthen his position in the minds and hearts of his fellow Hebrews he was met with a sneer of envy and suspicion, instead of an expression of gratitude and confidence. The report of his act the day before had indeed spread among his people, but instead of finding them cherishing it hopefully and looking upon him as another Joseph, he was shocked to discover that they were spreading it enviously and looking upon him as a conceited and arrogant son of luck who took pleasure in his assumed authority.

2. Flees to Midian

With his dream castles crashing around him, his mother's prayers coming to naught, and the immediate danger of the report getting to Pharaoh's ears, Moses fled the country. He must have remembered Joseph's experience of being snatched out of a position of high favor in Potiphar's house and cast into prison. If that had happened to Joseph when he was innocent, what chance would he have, when his guilt could be proved quite easily? As he went on his way, Moses must have concluded that the Lord had not intended that he should be a deliverer after all. That high calling would come to another. In the meantime, he would get out of the country until his rash deed should be forgotten.

IV. CALL AND COMMISSION (Ex. 2:23 to 4:31)

In the land of Midian, Moses found safety and seclusion in the home of a shepherd priest. He married one of the man's daughters and settled down to a quiet home life. While shepherding his sheep, Moses got acquainted with the wilderness area through which he was to lead Israel forty years. He learned the location of good watering places and stored up other information that was to be of great service to him later.

1. *Meditations in Midian*

Through the long days as he tended his sheep, Moses had ample opportunity to meditate upon his past. He must have felt that he had made a miserable failure of his life. With the promise of a brilliant career in Pharaoh's court, he had ruined it all in a rash effort to help his people. No doubt he thought that it would have been better if he had left them to their fate, while he cultivated his opportunities at the court. Probably he could have done more for them by speaking a friendly word for them to Pharaoh. But he had thrown away his opportunity. One of the best educated men of his day, he had blundered himself into the despised task of tending sheep. How his court friends would laugh if they could see him now!

2. *Called at the Burning Bush*

One day, as Moses had been musing thus on his failure and the miserable plight of his people, God spoke to him out of the burning bush. He was indeed to be the deliverer of his people, but not by his power or his ingenuity. It was to be by the power and wisdom of God. We are not surprised that, after these forty years of meditating upon his failure, Moses said: "Who am I, that I should go unto

Pharaoh, and that I should bring forth the children of Israel out of Egypt?" (Ex. 3:11). Had he not tried it once and failed? But this time God was to be with him, and he was to follow a plan of divine providence and not of human impetuosity.

God gave Moses the significance of the name "Jehovah" as a comfort and guide. "I am that I am" (Ex. 3:14) is his name, and that is to be remembered whenever he is called Jehovah. It points to his eternity and trustworthiness. Though conditions changed and men failed, he would remain their great God, eternally the same.

When Moses hesitated and asked for a sign, God gave him the sign of the rod that became a snake and of the leprous hand and finally the water that changed into blood.

3. Aaron Called to Help

Aaron, Moses' brother, was promised to him as a helper and spokesman. The brothers met as Moses was entering Egypt, and they went carefully over Moses' call and commission to deliver Israel from Egyptian bondage, and Aaron said that he had been called to help. And so they began their forty years of arduous labor together for Israel. They proceeded at once to call a meeting of the representatives of their people and to tell them of the divine call. After Moses and Aaron had exhibited their signs, the people believed. Was it because Moses did not have signs before that he had failed to elicit the confidence of his people, or was it simply that he was hastily following his own plan instead of seeking the Lord's? Perhaps it was the latter.

V. Contest with Pharaoh (Ex. 5–10)

Armed with the promise of Jehovah that he would be with them and with the assurance that their people believed in them, Moses and Aaron approached Pharaoh to make their amazing request known to him and the Egyptians. It was the essence of a revolution that they proposed when they asked the ruler to let the Hebrews depart from the country in which they were so entrenched as slave labor.

1. *The Issue*

If Moses entertained any notions of an early and easy victory, he was in for a speedy disillusionment. The Egyptian monarch had no intention of letting six hundred thousand excellent slave laborers get beyond his control. Haughtily refusing to take them seriously, the king sent Moses and Aaron away and at the same time issued the decree that the burden of the slaves should be made heavier by requiring them to find their own straw but make the same number of bricks.

The leaders in Israel then turned to Moses, putting the entire blame for their sad plight upon him. He did the only thing that he knew to do and the wisest thing that he could have done; he went to God in prayer about it. Then Jehovah prepared him for the ordeal that was ahead by telling him that Pharaoh would be stubborn and that the victory would be achieved only after a long struggle and only by the power of God. Therefore, Moses must speak to the children of Israel and prepare them for the contest that they might have patience and faith. Then he must go before Pharaoh boldly, in the confidence that Jehovah would be with him in sufficient power to deliver all the Israelites from their bondage.

Then the struggle was on, a struggle between the God of the Hebrews and the gods of the Egyptians, with Moses and Aaron representing Jehovah and the magicians representing the religion of Egypt. It was also to be a contest between obedient faith and fickle superstition. Pharaoh would not respond to reason; therefore, God resorted to miraculous intervention.

2. Rods and Snakes

The first encounter brought forward the sign of the serpent. When Aaron cast the rod upon the ground it became a snake. Then the king, accepting the challenge, sent for his magicians, who succeeded in making their rods look like snakes or their snakes look like rods. At that point it seemed that the contest was even, and that the magicians were as great as Moses. Just then Moses' rod-snake crawled over to the others and swallowed all of them, which was not only a sign of the superiority of Moses over the Egyptian magicians, but also indicated that the worship of Jehovah as represented by Moses was superior to the serpent-worship that they represented. It was done to impress Pharaoh, for he was to make the decision, but he dismissed it as a show and refused to listen further to the pleas of the slaves.

But it was not a show for entertainment. The rod that was used in discounting the pagan worship of serpents would be employed in bringing to light the vanity of other forms of false religion as practiced by the Egyptians.

3. Nine Plagues

The second encounter and the first plague came as Pharaoh was on his way to the Nile, the river that was sacred to Egypt. When Aaron stretched forth the rod, all the water in the land became blood. The fish died and a terrible stench arose, so that the river that had been worshiped now became abhorred by all. But again the king hardened his heart and refused to heed the cries of the slaves.

The plagues of the frogs, lice, and flies evidently pointed to the vanity of the worship of the scarab, a beetle that was reverenced by the Egyptians as the symbol of resurrection and fertility. When the lice came upon the people, the services in the Egyptian temples were automatically stopped, for it was a law among them that a priest could not take his place in the temple while he had lice on him. In each case the superiority of Jehovah was demonstrated over the gods of Egypt.

Then came the murrain upon the cattle, a direct challenge to the Apis-worship of Egypt. The sacred bull was their greatest god, the incarnation of the god of the lower world. If he had any power on earth at all, surely he would be able to protect the cattle! But, on the contrary, the murrain killed the cattle of all Egypt, with the exception of the land of Goshen.

There was a belief among the Egyptians that they could check the spread of evil by sprinkling ashes from the altar toward the sky. To expose the weakness of such a belief, Moses signalized the coming of the sixth plague by that sign. When the boils came upon the people they saw that their ceremony could be used by the true God to produce the opposite effect.

Then came the hail, the seventh plague, to rebuke them for their worship of the elements and to prove to them that Jehovah is supreme over all the forces of nature. This was followed by the locusts, indicating that the pest that they were in the habit of attributing to their gods was really under the power of Jehovah. The plague of the darkness was a rebuke to their worship of Ra, the sun-god. They believed that he brought forth the light of the midday sun, but where was he when the darkness continued in the land? It was Jehovah, the God of Israel, who decreed the darkness and three days later suspended it. He makes the light to shine. He is to be worshiped, and not the sun.

Each time Pharaoh relented, but his repentance was born of a fear that quickly subsided when the immediate danger was removed. It was not the true repentance that is a change of the mind and heart toward God, carrying the surrender of the life to him. Pharaoh was like a multitude of others who pray for deliverance in time of trouble and then forget God when the trouble has passed. He was also like many others in that his skepticism was mainly of the heart and not of the head. He refused to believe because he did not want to obey God, and that is true of the average skeptic. There is a vast difference between the superstition of Pharaoh and the faith of Moses.

These contests must have been of tremendous value to Moses in strengthening his faith and in preparing him for future hardships. They were valuable also to the Israelites. Out in the wilderness, tempted to give up and quit, their courage was to be strengthened by remembering their deliverance from Egypt.

VI. THE PASSOVER (Ex. 11:1 to 13:16)

Throughout the plagues there was a marked contrast between the effect on the Egyptians and that on the Hebrews. From the fourth plague on, the Israelites were exempted from the ravages of the pestilences that fell upon the land; consequently, they were enjoying a progressive peace and contentment, while their oppressors were experiencing increasing suffering. This gave the Israelites the opportunity that they needed to get everything in readiness for the departure from the land of their bondage.

1. *The People Prepared*

One last stroke of Providence was to fall upon the Egyptians to prove to them that Jehovah is the only true and living God, and to make Pharaoh let God's people go. This time it was to be a visit of death to every Egyptian home, including Pharaoh's, showing that Jehovah alone exercised complete control over all life. Ample warning was given to Israel so that the prescribed preparations might be made. They were to gather their possessions, their flocks and herds, and make ready for travel. At an appointed time they are to sprinkle the blood of a slain lamb on the doorpost of each house, so that the death angel might pass over them.

It was the zero hour for Israel. Behind them lay the long years of bondage, before them the beginning of freedom; behind them the agonizing cries of an enslaved people, before them the birth of a nation. Old things were passing away, and a new day was about to dawn, the first day of the first year of their calendar, and ever after it was to be a great memorial day (Ex. 12:14).

2. *The Passover*

Thus the Feast of the Passover was established. Three things are to be noted about it: (1) It was appointed of God, as his way to accomplish the deliverance of his people, and therefore it was accepted by him when kept in faith. (2) It was rooted in the needs of the people historically, but it also symbolized the people's need of God in every generation; they were not to be a self-reliant but a God-trusting people. (3) A blood sacrifice was provided as a substitute for the first-born of the people, thus symbolizing the substitutionary atonement that is at the heart of the Bible doctrine of redemption and that culminated in Christ's voluntary and sacrificial gift of himself for the sins of the world. "For our passover also hath been sacrificed, even Christ" (1 Cor. 5:7). When we observe the Lord's Supper we are keeping the Feast of the Passover as it has been fulfilled in our Saviour's death.

The command that each family should sprinkle the blood on the doorpost constituted a test of faith for the Israelites. It was the moment for every family to decide whether to risk everything on faith in God's promises or to continue in bondage to Pharaoh; whether to follow after liberty in an untrodden path or to follow in the well-worn path of slavery; whether to be the children of God in a world-redeeming service or to live and die as the slaves of Pharaoh. Each one had to decide in the family council. It was an act of faith and obedience for every Israelite.

3. *Deliverance*

At midnight a cry went up from the land of Egypt, a mighty cry that began with the first discovered dead child and swelled with tremendous crescendo as family after family learned of its sorrow, until the whole nation travailed in grief. The Israelites alone were not weeping, for they had been spared. When Pharaoh heard of this he sent his messengers to them urging them to go at once. And they arose and started on the great journey, six hundred thousand men, not counting the children, driving their cattle and sheep as fast as possible, carrying their babies in their arms, a pack on the back of every person old enough to carry a burden. What an exodus! What a venture of faith! Where could they possibly go? They had been in Egypt for hundreds of years, and so they had no land to claim as their own. What could they do? They were a simple shepherd people, venturing to lay aside their slave rags and put on the clothes of free men and walk away from the mighty kingdom of Egypt.

FOR CLASS DISCUSSION OR FURTHER STUDY

1. What is your evaluation of Moses' first attempts to deliver his people? What was right about his choice and motive (Heb. 11:24)? What was wrong with his plan?
2. Show how God used the events of the first eighty years of Moses' life to prepare him to be the deliverer of his people.
3. Discuss the process by which Pharaoh's heart became increasingly harder. Count the times that the account says that God hardened Pharaoh's heart and the times it says that Pharaoh hardened his heart. How do you reconcile the two statements?

CHAPTER 8

8

Moses the Lawgiver

Exodus 13:17 to 23:33

I. CROSSING THE RED SEA (Ex. 13:17 to 15:21)

At early dawn on the fifteenth of Nisan (corresponding to March–April) the Israelites set out upon their journey. It was understood among them that they were to start early in the morning, although they had been told not to leave their homes before day (Ex. 12:22). They were dressed and packed, ready to go, and so by families and small groups they left the land of bondage and started on their march to liberty.

1. *From Raamses to Succoth*

They had evidently agreed upon Raamses as the meeting place and Succoth as the first stop, and the leaders had been instructed in the plan of organization. As the groups came up, they were placed in columns by tribes and families and urged onward as rapidly as possible. Knowing the fickleness of Pharaoh as he did, Moses felt that there was no time to be lost. If Pharaoh should pursue them he would come in chariots, and it would be easy for him to overtake the walking multitude.

2. *Cloud and Fire for Guidance*

The pillar of cloud went before them by day and the pillar of fire by night. Thus did Jehovah indicate to them when and whither they should move and when and where they should camp. From Succoth it seemed that they were about to take the regular route of travel between Palestine and Egypt, the way that Jacob and his sons probably came down into Egypt. But that was not to be. They had many things to learn before they would be ready to enter the Promised Land. For one thing they were not sufficiently trained to go up against the mighty Philistines, and if they should meet them right soon the Israelites would become frightened and either turn back to Egypt or surrender to the Philistines and become their slaves. They must also receive the laws by which they were to be governed as God's people. Furthermore, they needed time to meditate and get better acquainted with God. As it was necessary for Paul to go into Arabia after his conversion, so it was necessary for Israel to go into the wilderness after the Exodus.

3. *Pursued by the Egyptians*

By a sudden change of direction to the south, God soon led them to Pihahiroth between Migdol and the sea. There they camped. A lookout noticed a cloud of dust out on the horizon and sensed that it was Pharaoh coming against them with his army. Once more the king had suffered a moral relapse; his repentance had drifted from him as quickly as the necessary formalities of the nationwide funeral were over, and now he was driving hard to overtake his slaves and force them to return to their labor. No doubt, as he urged his horses on, he was planning to add yet more to the burdens of the Hebrews. He would teach them that they could not trifle with Pharaoh and the gods of Egypt! He would double again the number of bricks that they would be required to make and let them continue to find their own straw!

The lookout rushed to Moses, shouting that the Egyptians were coming. But that meek man was not overwhelmed with the report; in fact, he expected it, for he was a man of prayer and therefore he was ready for the emergency. The people became excited and frightened as the news spread like a forest fire through the camp. They were trapped, they thought, between the sea and the desert, with the Egyptians riding hard upon them from the rear. What could they do? Only one thing, said Moses, and that was to trust in God. They were not able to deliver themselves, but man's extremity is always God's opportunity, provided man trusts God. Jehovah would make one last demonstration before them of his supremacy over the gods of the Egyptians. Thereafter they should never be able to doubt his willingness and power to save them in any experience of need.

4. Miraculous Passage

The pillar of cloud came between the two camps, putting the Egyptians in darkness, but there was a silver lining to that cloud on the Israelites' side, and they had light. Then, at God's decree, a mighty wind made a path through the bed of the sea for the fleeing slaves, and they went across with their families and their flocks and herds. No sooner were they on the opposite shore than the Egyptians discovered that they had fled from their camp into the sea. Confident that they could go anywhere these slaves could, Pharaoh's forces drove pell-mell into the bed of the sea. But God caused the wind to change, the tide came in, the heavy chariots began to sink in the sand and water, and soon the mighty army was a swirling mass of frantic men and horses, as they struggled to save themselves from the watery grave (see Psalm 77:16-20).

On the other shore God's people stood speechless. It was Jehovah's hour, and no time for them to talk. They were awed by the scene, which was a majestic display of divine power. They had triumphed over their enemies, and yet they had not done a thing but obey God's command. Then they broke forth into song, led by Moses and Miriam, praising Jehovah for his goodness in delivering them from the Egyptians. This poem of Moses is probably the oldest in the world, and for sublimity of conception and grandeur of expression remains one of the greatest. Turn to it now and read it through (Ex. 15:2–19).

5. *Important Lessons*

As we pause here there are at least four important lessons that come to us out of this Red Sea experience: (1) Take every problem to God in prayer. (2) If God commands us to go forward in danger, we may know full well that he will lead us safely through. (3) When we are faced with danger we should first seek to determine whether we are there because of our selfish interests or in obedience to God's command. If we go into danger thoughtlessly, it is rashness; if we go into it wantonly, it is foolhardiness; but if we go into it because only thereby can we follow our Master and do what he commands, this is true courage, and at such times we shall always find him at our side. (4) After deliverance we should be grateful.

II. ON THE MARCH (Ex. 15:22 to 17:16)

As they turned away from the sea, the Israelites must have experienced a new feeling of security and independence as a people. In the brief space of a night, they had been marvelously delivered from the danger of further attack at the hands of the Egyptians. They had passed from Africa into Asia, from bondage into liberty. They were now on their way to the Promised Land and a career of service. Immediately before them stretched the level plains of the Arabian desert, where their fathers had wandered in former times and where Moses had fed the flocks of his father-in-law. There was no need to hurry now. With the Egyptian army out of the way they could proceed leisurely, allowing time for the animals to graze and the people to find food as they went on their way.

1. *Marah*

After three days of marching in the wilderness of Shur without finding good water, they came to Marah. Here there was plenty of water but it was bitter, and the people murmured, but Moses prayed about it. When he had followed the answer to his prayer and the water had been made tasty, he brought to them a special word from the Lord: "If thou wilt diligently hearken to the voice of Jehovah thy God, and wilt do that which is right in his eyes, and wilt give ear to his commandments, and keep all his statutes, I will put none of the diseases upon thee, which I have put upon the Egyptians: for I am Jehovah that healeth thee" (Ex. 15:26). This was the beginning of the covenant at Sinai, for it embraced in principle all that was ultimately given. It pledged the people to receive and obey all that the Lord should later command. On his part God promised to protect them from calamity. Deliverance increases our obligation to God and brings the assurance that he will deliver us again in our future times of trouble.

2. *Elim*

The next recorded stop was at Elim, where there were twelve springs of water. Thence the Israelites came to the wilderness of Sin. They had been on the march about six weeks, and their food supply had been used up. Tired and hungry, they began to compare their present lot with the conditions under which they had lived in Egypt. Their fickle and short memories recalled only the fact that they had food there, while they forgot the burdens and oppression.

3. *Bread and Meat*

Providing food for a multitude of nearly two million people was no small problem. What was Moses to do? They could not wait to plant crops, even if they had enough fertile ground around the camp, for the people would starve long before harvesttime. Someone says that they should have eaten the cattle and sheep which they had, but all that they had would probably not have lasted more than a few days, or a few weeks, at best. Then, too, the flocks and herds probably did not belong to all the people in common, but to a small group who had managed to prosper and save something in the last years of bondage. There was simply no way for Moses to provide enough food at once. Then the question became, What would God do? The situation could be saved only by a miraculous answer to prayer.

While the people complained and Moses prayed, God once again wrought their deliverance. In the mornings they were given manna, a bread-like substance that came like dew on the ground with every new day except the sabbath, and in the evenings the camp and surrounding ground swarmed with great coveys of quail. The people had only to go out and gather the food. They were fed by the grace of God. The gift of the manna continued for forty years and remained for centuries in the thought of the Hebrews as one of the greatest signs of God's presence with them. It was often referred to for the encouragement of the people and used in their prayers of gratitude and praise (Neh. 9:15). On one occasion when the Jews asked Jesus for a sign they reminded him of the account in the Scriptures concerning the manna, that God, "gave them bread out of heaven to eat" (John 6:31).

4. Rephidim

From the wilderness of Zin Moses led the people to Rephidim, but there was no water for them to drink. True to the habit that they had early formed, they complained to their leader, reminding him that they had food and water in Egypt and blaming him with their present hardship. In vain he reminded them that Jehovah was still their God and that they were really tempting him. But that only added to their peevishness, and they became so excited that they threatened to stone their leader. Moses took the matter to the Lord in prayer, and water was miraculously provided.

5. *The Amalekites*

Their next problem was their first military encounter. The Amalekites challenged their right to pass through that country, and the Israelites had to defend themselves in battle. The people of Amalek were an old nation, for we have a reference to them as a nation in the earlier life of Abraham (Gen. 14:7), and as "the first of the nations" (Num. 24:20), and a suggestion in another place that they had at one time held Palestine (Judg. 12:15).

Moses had discovered Joshua as a courageous and capable leader, and he gave to him the task of selecting and training an army and leading against the enemy. While the battle was on, Moses and Aaron and Hur stood on the top of a hill, watching and praying. Moses stretched forth his hands, holding the rod that had been the symbol of God's presence and miraculous power, and the Israelites gained their first victory.

III. A GOOD FATHER-IN-LAW (Ex. 18)

As the Israelites came toward the wilderness of Sinai, the report of their presence in the vicinity and their victory over the Amalekites was brought to Jethro. Probably Moses sent a messenger to him inviting him to come for a visit, bringing his daughter, Moses' wife, and their two sons with him. (Moses had evidently sent his wife and sons back to Midian after starting to Egypt with them. Compare Exodus 4:18–26 with 18:1–4.) Moses went out to meet his relatives as they approached his camp and greeted them warmly. Then, as they made themselves comfortable in his tent, he recounted his experiences since he had left them in Midian, dwelling at length on the miraculous way in which Jehovah had delivered his people again and again.

1. *Jethro Advises Moses*

Jethro, apparently a believer in Jehovah, rejoiced with his son-in-law in the signal victories that God had given through his leadership and joined with him in a special sacrifice of thanksgiving. Then came the elders of Israel to welcome their leader's father-in-law with a feast.

The routine of the camp was not interrupted for long, and soon Moses was once more absorbed in the multitudes of duties in molding his people into a nation. While his father-in-law sat nearby, he labored all through the day with the problems that the people brought to him, and at the close of the day he was completely exhausted. Jethro noticed that the lines were deepening on Moses' face, and he began to wonder what the children of Israel would do without their leader. If this daily grind kept up, he would surely not last much longer, and the people were not yet sufficiently trained to go forward without him. Jethro set his mind to work on the matter, for it seemed to him to be of primary importance.

And so it came to pass, as they sat in front of the tent at the close of the day, that the priest of Midian undertook to give his son-in-law a bit of advice. He suggested that Moses organize the people into groups of thousands, hundreds, fifties, and tens, with a judge over each group, and the judges would relieve him of a great mass of the detail work. The problems could be classified into minor, middle, and major cases. The elementary matters could be handled by the first judge who had a group of ten; certain other questions would be brought to the judge of fifty; the problems that were more complex could be brought to the judge of a hundred, or of a thousand. The matters that could not be handled satisfactorily by these judges or that were immediately classified as of major importance were brought to Moses. In other words, here we have the simple outline of the plan of courts that has been followed in many nations since. In our country we have the magisterial, county, circuit, and Federal courts. It came to us from Moses, and he got the idea from his father-in-law.

2. Greatness Demonstrated

Indeed, here were two noble characters; Jethro was smart enough to see a simple solution to a complex problem, and Moses was big enough to accept his advice and act upon it. Moses was meek in his relations with his father-in-law as well as with his God, and he was a greater leader for his meekness. What do you suppose would have been the outcome if Moses had resented Jethro's advice and regarded it as presumption to think that any outsider could tell him how to handle his people? Moses might have reminded his father-in-law that he had led them with some measure of success so far without advice from outsiders. There are plenty today who react in that manner to friendly advice. The result might have been that Moses would have died before his important work as lawgiver and prophet was finished. We may well thank God today that he had sense enough to accept good advice.

Another mark of greatness in Moses was his concern to give Jethro full credit for the institution of this splendid system of judging. Evidently that was the only reason he had for including the visit of his father-in-law in the account that he wrote of the experiences of this period. A weaker and more selfish person might have used the plan and then taken full credit for the results achieved.

IV. THE COVENANT AT SINAI (Ex. 19–20)

It was approximately a year after Moses received his call at the burning bush that he found himself right back in the same locality, around Mount Sinai, at the head of a multitude of people. Hitherto had Jehovah led him, even as he said he would. But what of the future? Where would they go from here? This was not the Land of Promise that figured in the covenant with Abraham. What was he to do now? According to his habit he took his problem to the Lord in prayer. We can imagine that he sought the same spot where God had spoken to him out of the burning bush and that he removed his sandals from his feet as he had done before and prayed alone, asking his God to tell him what he should say to his people.

1. A Covenant Sealed with Blood

The answer to the prayer came: "Thus shalt thou say to the house of Jacob, and tell the children of Israel: Ye have seen what I did unto the Egyptians, and how I bare you on eagles' wings, and brought you unto myself. Now therefore, if ye will obey my voice indeed, and keep my covenant, then ye shall be mine own possession from among all peoples: for all the earth is mine: and ye shall be unto me a kingdom of priests, and a holy nation." (Ex. 19:3-6.) They formed a holy covenant, sealed with blood (Ex. 24), pledging their abiding allegiance to Jehovah, while he promised to be with them as long as they obeyed him.

2. The Ten Commandments

It was to be a covenant of law, that the people might know the will of their God and do it. The first fundamental statement of law is given in the Decalogue, the Ten Commandments, which may be divided into two groups.

The first group deals with the relationship of the people to God and embraces the first four Commandments. The first commands monotheism, the worship of only one God, Jehovah. Other gods are no gods at all. They are not to be worshiped. The second forbids idolatry. God is spirit and not to be worshiped through images or pictures. The third forbids profanity. God's name is holy and is not to be made common among sinful men. The fourth commands observance of the sabbath as holy, for it is God's day.

The other group deals with the social relationships of the people. The fifth commands respect and honor for parents, placing divine recognition upon the home as the fundamental unit in human society. The sixth forbids murder, recognizing the sanctity of human life. God gives life, and only God should take it away. The seventh forbids adultery, commanding purity of relations between men and women. The eighth forbids stealing, recognizing the right of every individual to the possession of property. The ninth forbids slander and gossip. The tenth forbids covetousness, commanding the control of the desires of the heart with reference to the possessions of another.

3. *Importance of the Commandments*

These Commandments were to be the foundation of all the laws to be given to Israel. As Dr. Sampey suggests, they may be regarded as Israel's constitution, all else in the Pentateuch comprising the statutory law.[1] In first setting forth the Commandments that cover man's direct relations with God, the principle is laid down that religion is the foundation of morality. Man's first duty is to love God and serve him supremely, and the second obligates him to love his fellow man and to live for his welfare.

The civilized world recognizes the primary importance of these laws. They have not been repealed in the thinking of people, but have been made the foundation of all systems of law. Our task is not to improve upon them, but to observe and obey them. Jesus interpreted them as applying to the motives of the heart as well as to the deeds of the life. He said murder begins with hatred, adultery begins with lust, and so all the words of the Decalogue point to the condition of man's heart.

The purpose of the Decalogue was to provide a basis of molding the people into a national unity. If the wisdom of Jethro was to bear fruit it must be subordinated to the wisdom of Jehovah, and the commandments of God must be the pattern of principles on the basis of which judgment was to be rendered. If there was uniformity of thought among the people about duties to God and to one another, they would be a united people. The Decalogue was also given to provide a basis on which all future legislation would be given and on which the people would realize the progressive development of God's plan of redemption. The revelation and redemption in Jesus Christ did not abrogate the Ten Commandments, but expanded them into a spiritual relationship that cannot become a reality apart from him.

V. CIVIL LAW (Ex. 21–23)

In making specific applications of the commandments in the Decalogue, the civil and religious laws were given through Moses. We may consider the first here, and leave the second group for the last chapter.

In Exodus 21 to 23, the ordinances point mainly to the regulation of the civil and social life of the Israelites, although scattered throughout there are ordinances that have to do with religious ceremonies. In some of the other chapters, such as the thirty-fourth, civil ordinances are given in connection with other prescriptions. Our concern here is not so much to get them arranged according to the time when they were given, but to seek to understand the meaning and purpose.

These ordinances deal with the treatment of slaves (21:2–11, 20, 21, 26, 27); murder or manslaughter (21:12–15); kidnaping (21:16); treatment of parents (21:17); responsibility for injuring another person (21:18–19, 22–25); responsibility for thievery and property damage (21:28 to 22:15); sexual immorality (22:16–19); treatment of widows, orphans, and strangers (22:21–24); lending of money (22:25–27); justice and fair treatment of neighbors (23:1–9); and the sabbath and agricultural laws (23:10–12). Along with these three chapters one should study Deuteronomy 20 to 25, where some of these laws are restated and others are added.

VI. The Law Through Moses

Whence came all of these laws? Out of the mind of Moses? Out of his knowledge of Egyptian legislation? He always insisted to his people that they came from God. When he spoke to them he began by saying that God had told him what to say to them. When he wrote an account of the laws he attributed them to God. Certain it is that the impression was made on all Israel for all time to come that the law was not from Moses, but through Moses from God. "For the law was given through Moses; grace and truth came through Jesus Christ" (John 1:17).

But how did it come from God through Moses? How did the human ruler get it from the divine Ruler? The answer is, through prayer. Moses was in prayer every time Jehovah spoke to him. He went up into the mountain, his prayer place, to commune with his Lord and to secure guidance in the tremendous task that was before him, and when he came back he had a message for the people concerning God's will that should be their law.

FOR CLASS DISCUSSION OR FURTHER STUDY

1. What lessons do we gain from the account of the crossing of the Red Sea?
2. Cite the ways in which God supplied various needs of his people after the deliverance at the Red Sea. What conclusions may we draw about how God always deals with the needs of a people who are advancing under his guidance?

[1] John R. Sampey, *The Heart of the Old Testament* (Nashville: Broadman Press, 1922), p. 77.

CHAPTER 9

I. INTERCEDING FOR ISRAEL (Ex. 32–34)

    1. Worship of the Calf
    2. Jehovah's Wrath and Moses' Prayer
    3. Moses' Wrath and Intercession
    4. Face-to-Face Talk
    5. The Shining Face

II. ERECTING THE TABERNACLE (Ex. 24–27; 30–31; 35–40)

    1. Willing Gifts
    2. Significance of the Tabernacle

III. THE PRIESTHOOD UNDER AARON (Ex. 28–29, 39)

    1. Priests and Prophets
    2. The Levites
    3. Support of the Priests and Levites

IV. OFFERINGS AND SACRIFICES (Lev.)

    1. Significance and Purpose
    2. Two Classes of Sins
    3. The Day of Atonement

V. WILDERNESS WANDERINGS (Num.)

    1. The Move from Sinai
    2. Family Jealousy
    3. The Failure at Kadesh-barnea
    4. Dreary Wandering
    5. Sin of Moses

VI. MOSES' FAREWELL MESSAGES AND DEATH (Deut.)

    1. Three Addresses
    2. A Great Prophet
    3. Departure and Death

9

Moses the Prophet

Exodus 24–40; Leviticus, Numbers, Deuteronomy

THE HEADINGS for these last two chapters should not be taken as indicating a break in the experience of Moses when he ceased to be the lawgiver and became the prophet, for all that he did in speaking for God to Israel designated him as a prophet. Many of the strictly religious and ceremonial laws were given at the same time that the civil and moral laws were declared. But in this last period he was pre-eminently the prophet.

I. INTERCEDING FOR ISRAEL (Ex. 32–34)

At the command of Jehovah, Moses again went up into the mountain, leaving Aaron and his two sons and seventy elders to take charge of the people until he should return. He remained away from the people so long that they began to wonder whether he would ever return.

1. *Worship of the Calf*

The religious fervor of the people and their gratitude to God for all his blessings began to wane, and they talked of what they would do without Moses. They knew the religion of Egypt better than the true worship of Jehovah, and soon their minds were recalling the wild orgies that so frequently took place in the Egyptian temples, and then some one suggested that they might have a service like that out here in the wilderness. The suggestion was brought to Aaron, and he agreed, probably thinking that he would not be forsaking the worship of Jehovah but merely giving the people a visible symbol to make the service more real to them. It was against just this sort of thing that one of the Commandments was given, but the people had forgotten those sacred injunctions for the time being.

Miriam led a group of the women in playing on their musical instruments and singing, while others presented the vulgar dances of the Egyptians, and the rest of the people gave themselves over to unrestrained indulgence in the heathen rites before the image of the calf.

2. *Jehovah's Wrath and Moses' Prayer*

Jehovah's wrath was kindled against them and he let Moses know that he would be willing to destroy the children of Israel and begin over again with him and his children. But Moses prayed for them, reminding God of the great things that he had already done for them and of the impression that had been made on the Egyptians by the miraculous deliverance from bondage. If the Israelites should be destroyed in the wilderness, the Egyptians would say that the God of the Hebrews was not able to take care of them after delivering them.

3. *Moses' Wrath and Intercession*

Feeling that his prayer had been answered and that Jehovah had turned his wrath aside, Moses went down to the camp. As he came into full view of the wild scene, his own anger broke loose. He threw the stone tablets upon the ground, breaking them, and then he burned the golden calf and cast the ashes on water and made the people drink it. After leading the Levites on a bloody trail of vengeance and atonement, he went back to the mountain to pray.

Broken in heart because of the sins of the people, Moses cried out to God to forgive them. He is the magnificent man of prayer here, more like Jesus in Gethsemane than any other figure in the Old Testament. He put himself on the altar as a sacrifice for the people. "Forgive their sin;" he prayed, "and if not, blot me, I pray thee, out of thy book which thou hast written" (Ex. 32:32).

4. Face-to-Face Talk

The prayer was heard and the sins forgiven, as the people were led into a prolonged period of mourning and repentance. And Moses came to know God in more intimate fellowship. It is said now that "Jehovah spake unto Moses face to face, as a man speaketh unto his friend" (Ex. 33:11). It is significant that Moses did not attain to such a high place of spiritual experience with God until after he entered into his self-sacrificing prayer of intercession for his people. It was said of Job that the Lord turned his captivity when he prayed for his friends (Job. 42:10). God is our Redeemer and we do not know him intimately until we know him in the redemption that is wrought through suffering and crucifixion. Paul prayed that he might know the Redeemer in "the fellowship of his sufferings" (Phil. 3:10).

Then Moses prayed for a further revelation of the majesty and glory of God, saying, "If thy presence go not with me, carry us not up hence" (Ex. 33:15). Following divine instructions, Moses carved two tables of stone to take the place of the ones that he had broken, with the Ten Commandments written on them. Then God appeared to him in an extraordinary manifestation of supernal glory.

5. The Shining Face

With the celestial afterglow of that transcendent experience lingering in his heart, Moses returned to his people. In his soul he knew that he would never be the same man after that visit with God, but he was not conscious of any change in his outward appearance. But the people noticed it at once. They always notice the change that genuine prayer makes in a person. The man of God may pray in secret, but he cannot keep secret the fact that he prays. The light of God's presence within will illumine the countenance without.

II. ERECTING THE TABERNACLE (Ex. 24–27; 30–31; 35–40)

One of the most pathetic parts of the incident of the golden calf was that while the people were donating their jewels to make a heathen image their God was instructing Moses in the plans and specifications for building the tabernacle, where they might assemble themselves for worship and prayer. The execution of those plans was interrupted by that deplorable lapse and its aftermath, but with all of that out of the way, their leader was ready to bring them to the appointed task.

1. *Willing Gifts*

The tabernacle and ark were to be provided out of the voluntary offerings that the people would bring. "Every man whose heart maketh him willing" (Ex. 25:2) was to bring an offering. Skilled workmen were chosen to do the delicate work and to supervise the labor of the others. The designs were wrought out carefully and all the parts and the fastenings and couplings were made separately and brought to Moses. Then on an appointed day the parts were assembled and the tabernacle and altars erected. It must have been a glorious day for the nation, when all the people co-operated in erecting the house of worship. And it was a marvelous exhibition of Moses' ability to organize and control his people.

2. *Significance of the Tabernacle*

What was the significance of the tabernacle for Israel at this period? There are at least three definite answers that may easily be found in the Scripture account. In the first place, it signified a step forward in the development of the religious consciousness of the nation. When they left Egypt the cloud was a temporary manifestation of the presence of God to them. But now the tabernacle indicated that God dwelt with them and was accessible to all. Formerly he came down on the mountain and spoke to them through Moses, but now the house erected to the worship of God indicated that he was also with them and a part of them, the very center of their national life.

In the second place, it signified that it was the will of Jehovah that there should be a central place of worship for all the people. There would remain certain forms of family worship conducted in the tents of the people, but all of that should be subordinate to the worship that they should render to God as a people. This gave them religious unity and solidarity, prevented disintegration of their faith, and provided a means of preserving the revelation that God had given to them. The tabernacle was the forerunner of the Temple, built in Solomon's day.

The third significance of the tabernacle is that it became for Moses the substitute for Mount Sinai. Hitherto he had spent much time on the mountain in prayer, receiving instructions from God for the people. Henceforth, he was to commune with God in the tabernacle, in the midst of the camp. From now on to the end of his life, he was to divide his time largely between talking with God inside the tabernacle and talking to the people before it.

III. THE PRIESTHOOD UNDER AARON (Ex. 28–29, 39)

With the provision of the tabernacle as the central place of worship, the need for an established priesthood to minister there was recognized at once. In fact, along with the instructions for the tabernacle and ark given on Sinai, Moses received directions for choosing, equipping, and consecrating a

class of priests who should be ready for the first service and
who should be the beginning of the order of priests to serve
in Israel perpetually.

1. *Priests and Prophets*

In all of the experiences of Israel to this point, Aaron,
Moses' older brother by three years (see Ex. 7:7), had taken
a subordinate place. But now he was given a permanent
position of prominence, for he was to be the high priest, and
his sons were to minister with him (Ex. 28:1). The work of
the two brothers was to be definitely divided. Moses was to
remain the chief leader of the people in all things, and Aaron
was to have the burden of caring for the regular sacrifices and
services. Here we see the beginning of the two orders of religious leaders in Israel that figure so largely in later history—
the prophets following after Moses as interpreters of the law
and spokesmen of Jehovah for the nation, and the priests following after Aaron as ministers in the ritual of worship.

2. *The Levites*

All the men of the tribe of Levi, the tribe of Moses and
Aaron, were appointed to assist Aaron and his sons in the
care of the tabernacle and the daily services there. Ever after
this the Levites were recognized as the servants of the people
at the central shrine, and the descendants of Aaron were the
priests. They were to devote all their time to maintaining the
religious services.

3. *Support of the Priests and Levites*

But how were the religious leaders to be supported with
the necessities of life? Certainly they were not left to chance,
or doomed to poverty. The offerings that were brought by the
people to the tabernacle were to be taken by the priests. Only
certain parts of the animals were used in the offerings, and
the other parts that were edible were used for food by the

priests. The tithes of increase were given by all the people to the Levites, who in turn gave a tithe of all that they received to the priests. In addition to all of this, there was the atonement money of half a shekel that every man twenty years old and over was required to give.

It can readily be seen that as Israel prospered the priests and Levites would benefit in proportion. There is little wonder that in the time of Jesus the priests were a wealthy class.

IV. OFFERINGS AND SACRIFICES (Lev.)

The book of Leviticus, named for the Levites, sets forth in detail the instructions of God to his people regarding their offerings and sacrifices. This book is part of the inspired Scriptures, which are "profitable for teaching, for reproof, for correction, for instruction which is in righteousness" (2 Tim. 3:16).

1. Significance and Purpose

The sacrifices prescribed in the book of Leviticus are the offerings of a saved people in worship and praise; not to secure redemption, but to express gratitude for it; not the sprinkled blood to redeem, but offerings to meet the needs of a saved people in their approaches to God their Saviour. The principle of the offering in general is devotion of man to God expressed in an outward act. In the offering man gives something of real value, thus testifying to the earnestness of his action. The offering represented the offerer, and in many cases was regarded as a substitute for him.

What was the purpose of each of the offerings? This may best be seen if we group them into two classes. The first includes the burnt-offering (chapter 1), meal-offering (chapter 2), and the peace-offering or thank-offering (chapter 3). All of these were presented on the brazen altar within the court of the tabernacle, and sin is not suggested in connection with them. It is the faithful Israelite seeking to express his devotion to Jehovah with an acceptable offering. It is an act of worship. The second class includes the sin and trespass-offerings (chapters 4 and 5), and here the sinner comes confessing his sin and seeking forgiveness.

2. Two Classes of Sins

What sins were to be expiated with such offerings? That question draws our attention to the fundamental distinction with reference to sins that runs throughout the ritual of the covenant. Two classes of sins were recognized: sins of weakness or ignorance, sins committed unwittingly or unintentionally; and sins of purpose and of premeditation, or sins of rebellion against the God of their covenant. For the first class an atonement was provided, but there was no sacrifice prescribed for the sins of the second class. The priests were required to make atoning offerings for themselves and then for the people, and individual Israelites conscious of having committed sins, brought their offerings, confessing their sins (Lev. 5:5).

3. The Day of Atonement

The tenth day of the seventh month was designated as the annual day of Atonement, when all the people would present themselves to God through the priests for cleansing from sin. At that time, and only at that time, would the high priest enter the holy of holies within the tabernacle. Having first made an offering for himself and the other priests for the atonement of their sins, he then offered a sacrifice for the people, that the blood might be a sign of their atonement and forgiveness. After the blood offering was completed, a goat, over whose head the sins of the people had been confessed, was turned loose into the wilderness, symbolizing the fact that God had removed the sins of the people.

What provision was made for the other class of sins—the sins of rebellion? No sacrifice is prescribed in the ritual of the covenant for such sins. But to understand that, we must remember that the fundamental condition of the whole covenant, upon which all the sacrifices are based, is faith in God and obedience to his will. Wilful sins violated that fundamental principle and automatically rendered the sinner outside the covenant and so beyond the reach of the sacrificial system that Jehovah provided for his people who would seek diligently to do his will.

Was there no way for sinners guilty of such sins of rebellion to secure forgiveness? Their only hope was to plead the mercy of Jehovah. In two different instances God heard the prayer of Moses on behalf of his sinful people (Ex. 32:7–14; Num. 12:9–14). Jehovah revealed himself to Moses in the mount as a "God merciful and gracious, . . . forgiving iniquity and transgression and sin" (Ex. 34:6–7).

V. WILDERNESS WANDERINGS (Num.)

The Israelites had now been around Sinai a little more than a year, and the time had been crowded with instruction from Jehovah through Moses concerning the welding of the people into the nation of God's choice.

1. The Move from Sinai

With the foundation of their national life now well laid, what should be the next experience of the children of Israel? A movement of the cloud over the tabernacle indicated that it was God's will that they should prepare to take up the march again toward the Promised Land. Moses tried to persuade his brother-in-law, Hobab, to go with them as a guide, for he knew the wilderness paths. Hobab refused at first, but evidently yielded and went with them (Judg. 1:16; 4:11).

Had the year at Sinai effected a change in the temperament of the people? Moses might well have started on this new part of their journey trusting fervently that they had outgrown their habit of complaining at every hardship. But if he cherished such a hope it was blasted during the first days of travel. The people murmured against God, and the fire of Jehovah burned in the camp until they cried out to Moses, who prayed for them and the fire abated (Num. 11:1–3).

When the burden of leading the people grew heavy again, Moses was told to choose seventy elders to stand by him and help him (Num. 11:16ff). The people moved along further, and when their meat supply gave out the quails were sent to them again, but this time a plague broke out among them to rebuke them for their greed (Num. 11).

2. Family Jealousy

Surely Moses had enough trouble without adding family quarrels! Nevertheless such trouble came in the jealousy of Miriam and Aaron with respect to the successes of their younger brother. Jehovah defended Moses to the brother and sister, and the divine wrath was manifested against them in the leprosy that came upon Miriam, indicating that she had probably been the instigator of the trouble. But Aaron interceded to Moses, and Moses prayed to God for his sister, and her disease was healed. Moses was different from his brother and sister in the matter of jealousy, as his treatment of Eldad and Medad showed (Num. 11:26–30).

3. The Failure at Kadesh-barnea

When the Israelites were encamped at Kadesh, they were very near the border of the Promised Land. How should they enter it and possess it? The first task would be to inform themselves concerning the condition of the land and the inhabitants, and then they would be able to map out a plan of conquest and a route to be followed. Accordingly, twelve spies were chosen, a man from each tribe, and sent to reconnoiter and study the land and the people (Num. 13).

After forty days the spies returned, bringing glowing reports of the country and samples of the fruit growing there; but ten of them were afraid of the inhabitants. All of the enthusiasm and faith of Caleb and Joshua fell on deaf ears, for the people believed the ten fearful spies, and their fear led them to their greatest national crisis. They murmured and talked rebellion, proposing to elect a leader in the place of Moses and return to Egypt. Then Moses, Aaron, Joshua, and Caleb fell down before them, pleading with them to turn from their evil thoughts and not rebel against Jehovah. But they grumbled all the more and threatened to stone Moses and the other three with him. It was indeed a crisis for Israel as well as for Moses. What if they had been allowed to follow out their plans?

4. Dreary Wandering

Once again Jehovah intervened. The threatened uprising was quelled, and Moses the magnanimous prayed for the forgiveness of the people who had threatened to stone him. Here again he is the prophet of the type of Christ. His prayer was answered and the people were pardoned, but for their faithlessness they were condemned to wander in the wilderness until all the men from twenty years of age and up, who had feared to follow the Lord, had died. It would be necessary to rear a generation of men in the hard life of the wilderness before they would be strong enough to face the task of possessing the land.

Nearly forty years of wandering! It is a pathetic story. Death and mournings, murmurings, rebellions, and plagues make up the long and dreary story. One day it was defeat in battle, another it was the rebellion of Korah, yet again it was a plague.

The only advantage to come to them in all the years of aimless wandering in the wilderness was some further instruction in the law of Jehovah and in the proper conduct

of services by the priests and Levites, indicating that Moses
made good use of the time that the people wasted. While
they marked time, getting nowhere in their journey, he
prayed and studied and wrote, thus making real progress in
the purpose of God for his life. It may be that he wrote
the main part of the Pentateuch during these years of wandering.

At the beginning of the fortieth year after they left Egypt
they came again to Kadesh-barnea. Here Miriam, their sweet
singer, died and they mourned for her (Num. 20).

5. *Sin of Moses*

And how did Moses hold up under the strain of these forty
years of trying experiences? Nearly every day the people had
brought to him their individual problems and their com-
plaints as a nation. He had been governor, judge, preacher,
and pastor for them, as well as military strategist, protector
of health, and supervisor of food supplies. Day in and day
out they had nagged him. It is no wonder to us that his
patience gave way. In a fit of anger he sinned against Jehovah, Aaron participating with him in the sin. They were
forgiven; nevertheless their sin disqualified them for en-
trance into the Promised Land (Num. 20:2-13).

Shortly after this Aaron died at the age of one hundred
and twenty-three, and Eleazar, his son, became high priest
in his stead (Num. 20:22-29; 33:38-39).

When the fiery serpents came among them and many of
the people died, Moses was told to erect the brazen serpent
and the plague was stayed by the power of God in answer
to his servant's prayer. It was the type of the offering of
Christ on the cross (John 3:14).

After the experience with Balak and Balaam (Num. 22-
24), and the sin of the people before Baal-peor, followed
by the zealous intervention of Phinehas and the covenant of

an everlasting priesthood in him (Num. 25) and a second numbering of the people (Num. 26), Moses was warned of his approaching death (Num. 27), and Joshua was chosen as his successor.

VI. Moses' Farewell Messages and Death (Deut.)

Moses was now approaching the close of his career. Twice in recent months the shadow of death had fallen across his path, first in the going of Miriam and then of Aaron four or five months later. Added to that was the other burden of sorrow in knowing that he would not be permitted to go with his people into the Land of Promise. He had entreated Jehovah to let him go over into the land across the Jordan, but his request had been denied, and the Lord had said to him that he should not ask it again. He was permitted, however, to view the country from Pisgah's height (Deut. 3:23–28).

1. *Three Addresses*

In the last six weeks of his life Moses called the people together on stated occasions to hear what he would have to say to them. He knew that these would be his last words to them, and the people probably sensed it too. It must have been an inspiring scene: the old patriarch leaning on his staff with one hand while the other gestured toward the Promised Land and their future, the gentle breeze waving his snow-white beard and hair, while the people gazed upon him and listened to him entranced with his every word. He was an old man, yet he was vigorous and alert in mind and body. He had been their deliverer, lawgiver, and judge, but now he was their teaching prophet. What he said to them was by way of interpretation of their past experiences and prediction of what they might expect in the future, with warnings and admonitions mingled throughout.

The book of Deuteronomy comprises three main addresses: the delivery of the law to the priests, the charge to Joshua, and the great leader's farewell song and blessing, and then a brief statement concerning his death.

The first address (1 to 4) is mainly introductory, consisting of a brief rehearsal of the journey from Sinai to Kadesh and then the wanderings in the wilderness before their second arrival at Kadesh.

The second (5 to 26) gives some practical expositions of the law. Moses interprets all of it on the basis of love. They must love Jehovah and be jealous of his honor and zealous to obey him diligently in all things. The fourth and fifth verses of the sixth chapter early became a prominent part of their ritual. It may be heard today chanted frequently in the regular services of the Jewish synagogues and temples.

Moses told his people that, as he was teaching them, so they must teach their children the significance of their history as a people and the precepts of their God given at Sinai (chapter 6). He urged upon all of them the solemn duty of studying the law (chapter 11). And he told them that God would raise up before them a prophet like unto himself, unto whom they must hearken. We remember that Jesus told the Jews of his day: "For if ye believed Moses, ye would believe me; for he wrote of me" (John 5:46).

The third address (27 to 30) is occupied with instructions for the renewing of the covenant after they had entered the land beyond the Jordan. Here, as throughout all of the discourses, Moses admonished them to remember always to do God's will and keep his law, promising them that if they would follow in that path God would bless them and keep them by his power, but that if they forsook him and his ways he will deliver them over to their enemies. Let the reader pause just here and read the fearful consequences of disobedience that are pronounced in Deuteronomy 28.

2. A Great Prophet

Moses the prophet speaks through these addresses. The legislator and the judge, the deliverer and the historian, have faded into the background and in the soft glow of the eventide of his life he was pre-eminently the prophet. The many revelations from God mingled with his emotions and flowed in the alembic of one hundred and twenty years of experience. The shadows of sorrow and loneliness are blended with the scarlet flames of the burning bush and the brilliant light of Sinai when God walked by, as the masterful prophet with an inspired artistry of words painted scene after scene on the immortal canvas of the souls of his people. Now he pierced the law with spiritual intuition, interpreting it as love; again with inspired prescience he foretold their future.

Did Moses hit the mark when he attempted to predict their future? When he warned them of the evils of idolatry he put his finger upon their besetting sin through the centuries until the captivity. And when he admonished them against self-glorification he touched upon their besetting characteristic through the centuries after the return from exile. He told them that the only safeguard against all these dangers was to keep the spiritual fires burning in an abiding and singular devotion to Jehovah their God.

Moses' discourses ended, he finished his writing and delivered all the documents to the priests, with the instruction to read the whole law before the people every seven years (Deut. 31:9-13). Then he gave his charge to Joshua (31:23). Only one thing remained to be done before he would be ready to take his final departure: he wanted to gather the people together once more and give them a poem of praise to Jehovah that they might sing throughout their history, and then bestow his patriarchal blessing upon them. This he did with a display of poetical genius that fully matched his demonstration of other remarkable talents. (Read again Deut. 32–33.)

3. Departure and Death

Moses' work was done, his last instructive and inspiring messages had been delivered. It only remained now for him to make his departure. How would he leave them? Would they gather around him and weep on his neck, seeking to make a last atonement for the many times that they had made his work unnecessarily hard with their complaining and unfaith? Would they watch him then as he went slowly up the mountain for the last time, waving to him as he passed each turn in the path?

So far as we are informed by the account there was no formal leave-taking. Probably early one morning, before the coming of day had waked the sleeping host of Israel, Moses took Joshua and started up Mount Nebo, and as he came to the first high promontory he paused and looked down upon the camp. His people were just beginning to stir about with the morning duties, and as he looked upon them he put his hand on Joshua's shoulder and told him to go down and announce to the people that this was to be his deathday, and that they would not see his face again.

By the time the people had received the word from Joshua, Moses was on the top of Pisgah. As the morning sun bathed the land below him in dazzling light, God let Moses feast his eyes upon the land that was to be his people's possession. Hour after hour he looked through the hot tears of disappointment, then as the sun passed its meridian glory, his disappointment gave way to the peace and contentment of joyful resignation to the will of God, and as the slanting rays of the setting sun sent shadows lengthening across the hills and valleys, Moses sensed the eternal significance of the work that God had enabled him to do. In the quiet and beauty of his last earthly eventide, he walked with God to his eternal home.

"So Moses the servant of Jehovah died there in the land of Moab, according to the word of Jehovah. And he buried him in the valley in the land of Moab over against Beth-peor: but no man knoweth of his sepulchre unto this day" (Deut. 34:5–6).

FOR CLASS DISCUSSION OR FURTHER STUDY

1. Show why Moses is rightly called deliverer, lawgiver, prophet, intercessor.
2. Use a complete concordance and see if you can count over seventy times that Moses' name is mentioned in the New Testament. Read Hebrews 3:2–5 for an appraisal of Moses.

Questions for Review and Examination

CHAPTER 1

1. Why was the first man called Adam?
2. In what way was the creation of man distinguished from the rest of God's creative work?
3. What were the chief results of man's sin?
4. What do we know about Enoch? What do we learn from his life?

CHAPTER 2

5. What was God's ultimate purpose in calling Abram?
6. Why was Abram's name changed to Abraham?
7. Give an appreciation of Abraham's character.

CHAPTER 3

8. In what sense was Sarah the mother of the faithful?
9. How did Abraham go about getting a wife for his son?
10. How long were Isaac and Rebekah married before children came into the home? Why did Isaac favor Esau? Why did Rebekah favor Jacob?
11. Give a character sketch of Isaac.

CHAPTER 4

12. Tell how Jacob cheated Esau out of Isaac's blessing. How did the experience affect Esau?
13. Tell what you know of Rebekah.
14. What was the message of the dream that came to Jacob at Bethel? What bargain did he make with God?
15. What wages did Jacob receive during the years that he worked for Laban?

CHAPTER 5

16. Tell of the encounter when Laban overtook Jacob. What prayer at Bethel was now being answered?
17. Tell of Jacob's prayer at Peniel.

18. How did sin act as a boomerang in Jacob's life? What principle is demonstrated in this matter?
19. What were the outstanding events in the first seven years of Joseph's life? Characterize the next ten years.

CHAPTER 6

20. Tell of Joseph's periods of testing in Egypt and how he met each.
21. What successes did Joseph have in Egypt?
22. Why was the cup put into Benjamin's sack? What did Joseph's test prove?
23. How did Joseph receive his people? Where did they settle?

CHAPTER 7

24. What were some of the benefits derived from the bondage of the Israelites in Egypt?
25. What did the forty years of shepherding in Midian mean in preparing Moses for his future work?
26. What are three points of significance in the establishment of the Passover? In what way was it a test of faith?

CHAPTER 8

27. Describe the departure of the Israelites from Egypt. How were they led? What was the route?
28. How was the covenant established at Sinai?
29. What was the importance of the Decalogue in the life of Israel?

CHAPTER 9

30. State briefly the incident of the golden calf and tell what it revealed regarding Moses' character.
31. What was the significance of the tabernacle to the people of Israel?
32. Tell what happened at Kadesh-barnea. Show the significance of the choice of the people at that crisis.
33. What is the purpose of the addresses of Moses recorded in Deuteronomy?
34. Tell of Moses' death and burial.